Incentivizing Injustice

Incentivizing Injustice

The 2008 Financial Crisis and Prosecutorial Indiscretion

Sari Krieger

LEXINGTON BOOKS
Lanham • Boulder • New York • London

Published by Lexington Books
An imprint of The Rowman & Littlefield Publishing Group, Inc.
4501 Forbes Boulevard, Suite 200, Lanham, Maryland 20706
www.rowman.com

86-90 Paul Street, London EC2A 4NE

British Library Cataloguing in Publication Information Available

Library of Congress Cataloging-in-Publication Data

ISBN 978-1-7936-5449-6 (cloth)
ISBN 978-1-7936-5450-2 (electronic)

Contents

For Dad

List of Figures and Tables

FIGURES

TABLES

Introduction

After the $700 billion Wall Street bailout passed by Congress and signed by President Bush in October 2008,[1] millions of middle class and poor Americans who lost their homes or jobs were seething with anger. People were tired of a government that they believed favored Wall Street millionaires at the expense of ordinary people suffering on Main Street. By January 2011, four million families had lost their homes, another four and a half million were in danger of foreclosure.[2] The crisis resulted in 8.8 million jobs lost, 19.2 trillion[3] in household wealth gone and the worst recession since the Great Depression.[4] Later that year, the Occupy Wall Street movement sprang up in New York City, soon spreading across the country and propelled by the slogan, "We are the 99%." A few years later, these sentiments could be heard in the populist-fueled presidential campaigns of Donald Trump and Bernie Sanders. Even Hillary Clinton, hardly known for populist rhetoric, invoked the applause line "there should be no bank too big to fail and no individual too big to jail."[5]

In 2009, President Barack Obama and a Democratic majority in Congress swept into office on a wave of "hope" and "change." Initially, the Obama Administration was preoccupied with stabilizing the economy before addressing reform. Then in 2010, he signed into law the Dodd-Frank financial reform bill, which was intended to reduce the likelihood of a similar crisis occurring in the future. However, new regulations were not the only possible remedy for the ills of the crisis, nor were they the only action the public demanded. The American people wondered why no one prominent faced jail time. The federal government successfully criminally prosecuted forty-four bankers between 2010 and 2017, but none were responsible for the systemic failures of the financial crisis. They were largely executives from smaller banks, such as Brian Hartline, chief executive officer and president of NOVA Bank, and Gary Patton Hall, chief executive officer and president of Tifton Bank.[6] Certainly, none had the notoriety and power of a major bank CEO, whose demise would have a real chilling effect on criminal behavior in the industry and mollify public resentment.

Bankers and their institutions were already unpopular with the American public by the 2008 crisis. Polling shows that public confidence in banks drops after crises and economic downturns. Americans' confidence in banks dropped below 30 percent during the financial crisis of 2008 and as of 2016, had yet to recover. This is compared to 60 percent of Americans saying they have a great deal or quite a lot of confidence in banks in 1979, 51 percent in 1985 and 53 percent in 2004.[7]

A *CBS News MoneyWatch* column from September 2010 compared 2008 Wall Street executives with those of the Enron and savings and loan eras who could be seen making "perp walks." "Not so after the financial crisis. Forget perps - no one is even shouldering the blame, other than by engaging in the minor self-flagellation we've gotten from many of the prime suspects. These apologies, cheap as tin, are also couched in the ready alibi that while 'mistakes were made,' everyone made them. In that moral equation, collective guilt amounts to collective innocence."[8] A *Washington Post* blogger wrote in 2013 "Of the rogues' gallery who led the major Wall Street firms to the brink of the abyss, only to have a multitrillion-dollar taxpayer bailout pull them back, why have none become familiar with our nation's federal prison system?"[9]

Questions remained years after the crisis, as evidenced by this July 2017 headline from *The New Yorker*; "Why Corrupt Bankers Avoid Jail."[10] An October 27, 2020 *Bloomberg* editorial pondered why the Justice Department pursues impressive sounding but non-punitive monetary settlements, while earlier financial crises saw many executives facing jail time. Indeed, the *Bloomberg* piece discusses the mobster-style crimes committed by major bank executives, including money-laundering, fraud, and bribery. It decries the fact that companies pay billions in settlements as literal get-out-of-jail-free passes for its employees. *Bloomberg* advocates, as many others have long done, for mob-style prosecutions of these bank executives using racketeering statutes.[11] Even former Federal Reserve Chairman Alan Greenspan echoed these sentiments: "What the 2008 crisis exposed was a fragile underpinning of a highly leveraged financial system. Had bank capital been adequate and fraud statutes been more vigorously enforced, the crisis would very likely have been a financial episode of only passing consequence."[12]

All this rhetoric, and more generally the public anger and mistrust, suggest reasons for vigorous criminal prosecutions of major bankers. However, under the Obama Justice Department, none of these prosecutions took place. This is in stark contrast to earlier financial crises of the late twentieth century, such as the savings and loan crisis in the late 1980s and early 1990s, during which more than 1,000 executives were criminally prosecuted,[13] and the executives who were convicted during the accounting scandals of the early 2000s, with Enron's 22 leaders being the most prominent example.[14] Both of those crises saw executives criminally punished under Republican presidential administrations, while a Democrat, Barack Obama, saw no high-level executives face jail time on his watch. This defies conventional wisdom that Republicans are more pro-business than Democrats and therefore a Democratic administration would be more likely to prosecute finance industry executives. While these crises are not identical, they have some similarities that can be used as starting points for comparison in the quest for a satisfying explanation. In general, what we want to know, is why prosecutors make the decisions they do.

It is important to note that finance industry executives are not the only beneficiaries of the Justice Department's more recent tendency to settle rather than seek jail time for white collar criminals. For example, in October 2020, the Justice Department settled with Purdue Pharma LP and five members of the Sackler family, who are top company officials. The company, makers of the prescription opioid OxyContin, committed "reckless actions and violation of the law senselessly risked patients' health and well-being" according to a Justice Department press release.[15] Purdue, as a company, pled guilty in federal court to three felony counts for lying to regulators and paying doctors to push prescriptions of OxyContin in the years between 2007 to 2017. The Department press release boasts an $8 billion total settlement, constituting "the largest penalties ever levied against a pharmaceutical manufacturer." However, like the financial crisis executives, the Sackler family—actual human beings responsible for the company's actions - will serve no jail time and remain wealthy from the fruits of their illegal activity.[16] Congressmembers, along with some state attorneys general, opposed the Justice Department settlement, since although the Sackler family will have to pay $3 billion in restitution, they made more than $12 billion on OxyContin. Like during the financial crisis, the Purdue settlement means those that broke the law and harmed many Americans receive only a financial slap on the wrist. In a December 2020 Congressional hearing Rep. Jim Cooper of Tennessee told the Sackler family that he wasn't aware of any family in America "that's more evil than yours."[17] If a Sackler family member had killed someone personally, they would likely face jail time. However, as a business, they misled the public about a product that facilitated the recent opioid crisis, which has caused the deaths of 470,000 Americans over the past two decades.[18]

The American justice system loses legitimacy with citizens when there are separate consequences for the wealthy and everyone else. The consequences of this injustice and mistrust are very real. Although many factors led America to our current place of civic mistrust and threats to our very democracy, a strong case can be made for the massively uneven application of law enforcement in the wake of a devastating financial crisis that has had reverberations in society to this day. Let us seek to preserve our democracy and work toward a more just society. That effort requires us to first understand as best we can why the injustice has occurred.

Although many financial journalists, academics and others have asked why no systemically important executives faced criminal charges for the 2008 financial crisis, only a few have come up with anything approaching a compelling answer. In particular, Judge Jed Rakoff, journalist Jesse Eisinger and Duke University Law Professor Brandon Garrett have all been important voices and valuable sources. While there are similarities in this work and theirs, this book does not seek to reproduce their work. By focusing my argument on the specific institutional incentives for Justice Department attorneys doing the real work in complex, high-profile cases, I take a different approach. Ultimately, my hope is that I can add to the chorus of voices in search of a deeper understanding of prosecutorial discretion and the 2008 financial crisis.

EXPLANATIONS TO EXPLORE

Firstly, we must consider what even President Obama has said: "some of the most damaging behavior on Wall Street, in some cases, some of the least ethical behavior on Wall Street, wasn't illegal."[19] In evaluating this explanation, I will examine the elements of the crime of fraud. Although I can only speak in theory and in hindsight, can only rely on the public record, and don't have the pleasure of making those difficult cases in a court of law myself, I will make a series of arguments for individuals who may have been charged successfully by Justice Department prosecutors if they had the right incentives and resources to take such a risk. As the cliché goes, if you don't take risks, you can't win.

I will also consider the popular explanation that top bankers escaped prosecution because they are rich and powerful, and politicians do not bite the hand that feeds them. In evaluating this idea, I will explore whether finance executives sought to influence politicians across crises and political parties. Presidential influence over prosecutions is another popular explanation that I will consider. President Obama's leadership style was that of compromise, consensus, and caution, leaving him disinclined to take an aggressive stance on prosecutions and given to appointing individuals with a similarly cautious approach. Can the president really influence the decision of whether or not to prosecute? Donald Trump has illustrated for the public through his desire to prosecute his political enemies just how difficult that task is in the United States, even with loyal appointees. Beyond a direct order to prosecute, I will also discuss whether a president's appointment power and political party matter in finance executives potentially facing criminal charges.

Another explanation is that prosecutors were personally sympathetic to the bankers, viewing them as respectable high-status individuals who "made mistakes," rather than as potential criminals who violated laws. I will examine whether attitudes toward bankers have changed across the crises and consider generally this idea of "cultural capture." It could be said that cultural capture is simply a variation on traditional capture, or the power that wealthy individuals and groups have to control government actors. However, I argue that it deserves a separate treatment, as it goes beyond economic incentives and deals more with the human psyche. A fifth explanation is that the Justice Department, heavily invested in terrorism in a post–9/11 climate, lacked the resources necessary to defeat the extremely talented, experienced, and well-funded defense teams hired by the top bankers, and prosecutors did not want to proceed with half-measures.

My main explanation considers the incentives faced by prosecutors, both internal to the structure of the Justice Department itself and the personal incentives for future career prospects of these attorneys. I will discuss this idea first, and in its own chapter, as I believe it holds the most explanatory power. What happened in the years leading up to the crisis when the Justice Department was embarrassed by recent high-profile defeats shaped a culture of caution in the Department. Also, a lack of resources to make these cases likely played an important role in the disincentive to prosecute. Previous crises saw much more manpower and money devoted to interagency commissions to investigate arguably less complex financial crimes. As for personal incentives, prosecutors may have avoided risky criminal cases because they believed it would undermine future career prospects at top defense firms. This may be counterintuitive, as former federal prosecutors are a hot commodity at prominent white-collar defense firms. Those firms advertise their attorneys' history prominently on firm websites. However, what these firms want is a former prosecutor who has big wins, not a high-profile loss. A big swing and high-profile miss would also monopolize crucial years, leaving them with little else to impress a future private sector employer after a few years. As a safer alternative, prosecutors could rely on plea deals with impressive-sounding civil monetary penalties extracted from a bank, rather than pursuing a harder but more systemically important criminal case against individual executives responsible for fraudulent actions. In evaluating this explanation, I will consider the changing incentives they faced over time that made a private sector job even more attractive and give examples of this common career path.

To define the earlier crises for the sake of comparison, what I am calling the "Enron-era" crisis occurred in the early 2000s, when "creative" accounting and misrepresentation of company profits to shareholders for the financial benefit of executives plagued corporate America, resulting in fraud cases against executives of companies such as energy company Enron Corporation, telecommunications company WorldCom, cable television company Adelphia Communications Corporation, and security systems company Tyco International plc. Now defunct accounting giant Arthur Andersen was also involved in this crisis. The "savings and loan" crisis occurred in the late 1980s and early 1990s when more than 1,000 out of America's 3,234 savings and loan associations failed, partly due to fraudulent actions from their own officials.[20] While these two economic crises and the 2008 crisis were not the same in terms of economic scale and activities, what these three crises did have in common was economic losses for many Americans, a reverberation throughout the economy and regulatory and law enforcement challenges for the United States government. While acknowledging that these earlier crises may have been smaller and less complex, the similarities provide some point of comparison to ask why the earlier two saw successful criminal prosecutions of many systemically important corporate executives for fraudulent behavior that contributed to the crisis and nothing of the kind occurred in 2008. A question as large and looming as this one necessitates some explanation from the government. In the absence of a satisfying, or even an extensive explanation from government officials, I have sought to explore what we do know and to create a coherent narrative from it.

How will we even know who were the "bad guys" in the 2008 crisis, if any? As with any criminal case, the most important factor is not necessarily some objective truth, but what prosecutors can prove. I will lay out publicly available evidence for some of the 2008 crisis' worst executives, from those who ran companies that would give a loan to practically anyone with a pulse, to those whose employees joked their company would rate mortgage bonds created by cows. Government prosecutors with subpoena power could have potentially uncovered further proof of fraud beyond what is available to the public. However, without public disclosure of their efforts or strategies, we cannot know for sure. From this standpoint, I selected the starkest examples of fraud from the crisis based on information available in government documents, media reports and what I personally reported on as a journalist covering post-crisis litigation and regulation at a major media outlet. These cases include Lehman Brothers Chairman and Chief Executive Officer Dick Fuld, Countrywide Financial Chairman and Chief Executive Officer Angelo Mozilo, AIG Financial Products Chief Executive Officer Joseph J. Cassano, Citigroup executives, and rating agencies executives. Information from Clayton Holdings, a company that analyzed the quality of mortgages used in securitized mortgage products, was also used in support of a pattern of fraud. Based on those analyses, I proceed on the assumption that fraud did exist in 2008, but was not prosecuted, unlike the earlier crises.

A complicated problem rarely has a single and simple explanation. This one is no exception. There are many ways to view the question of why no high-level executives were criminally prosecuted, and therefore held accountable, for the 2008 financial crisis. While this book will focus primarily on a specific set of explanations, the seriousness of this question requires consideration from many perspectives. It is certainly possible that there simply was not fraud committed with enough evidence for a government prosecutor to prove in a criminal case, which has a much higher burden of proof than a civil proceeding. However, because prosecutors did not make enough of an attempt to bring these cases and skipped to settlement agreements, we may never know. The fact that we don't know whether enough evidence exists for criminal cases to have been made is precisely the problem. Ultimately, my argument is that even if fraud could likely have been proven by a skilled and brave prosecutorial team, all the wrong incentives were in place at the time for them to do so.

CRUX OF THE ARGUMENT

The main argument of this book is that changes inside and outside the Justice Department created an institutional structure that disincentivized government prosecutors to bring high-profile, risky cases. The government attorneys working on high-profile financial cases would likely be located in New York City, in the United States Attorney's Office in the Southern District of New York, which has a long track record of prosecuting the highest profile white-collar cases, and therefore has the most institutional experience. Alternatively, a case could have arisen from a district in Brooklyn, New York, Washington, DC, or parts of California—all places with extremely high cost of living. In comparison, many of the other United States Attorney's offices prosecute much less financially complicated, more parochial cases. One attorney called them "lobster cases," referring to the kinds of cases he saw during his temporary stint at a small New England U.S. Attorney's Office.[21]

These Assistant United States Attorneys (AUSA)—those hired rather than politically appointed—faced a change in both personal and institutional incentives over time. The cost of living in New York City is painfully high, as any resident knows all too well. Of course, an ambitious, smart AUSA *might* want to work in government service as a prosecutor for his or her entire career. However, we can hardly *expect* them to do so. The moral or emotional satisfaction of this career path has become an impractical and unlikely choice over the much more lucrative choice of switching after a few years of government service to a private defense firm position, and eventually partnership. These firms prize attorneys with prosecutorial experience. Top white collar defense firms boast in their staff biographies any government prosecutorial experience. However, they want to hire a prosecutor who can boast big wins, not big losses. Therefore, it's best for these attorneys to take what impressive-sounding wins they can get, and not gamble too much on a difficult bet.

In previous decades, the gap was much smaller between top federal prosecutor salary and what their private sector counterpart could earn as a partner. This change mirrors the time period when government prosecutors stopped being prosecutors and became negotiators. Settlement agreements with major banks and certain banking figures were standard practice for the 2008 crisis, while the previous crises saw a focus on prosecutions and jail time. The ability to make much more money in an outrageously expensive city would be a powerful incentive to be more cautious, seeking a safer and still impressive-sounding settlement agreement, rather than a more difficult and riskier prosecution. Firms want to see prosecutors who handled big name, complex cases, but not those who tried them and lost. Seeking settlement agreements is clearly the safer path for government prosecutors. They can garner headlines that sound like being tough on banks, splashing big dollar amounts on the news pages.

At the same time, the Justice Department experienced two major internal factors that only encouraged caution. In the early years of the new century, the Department experienced a series of high-profile embarrassments in white collar cases. For example, when energy company Enron Corporation collapsed due to a major accounting fraud scandal, the Department prosecuted its accounting firm Arthur Anderson for destroying incriminating documents. The firm subsequently went out of business due to reputational annihilation, leaving many innocent employees out of work. The United States Supreme Court later overturned the conviction on procedural grounds. The Department took much of the blame for destroying the company, rightly or wrongly. Settlement agreements are unlikely to put a company out of business like a criminal conviction. Therefore, the Department increasingly relied on them for the 2008 crisis. Somehow, a fear of holding individuals criminally accountable got lumped in with the more legitimate fear of prosecuting entire companies. Secondly, after the terrorist attacks of September 11, 2001, federal criminal justice resources in terms of budgets and manpower underwent a massive shift to counterterrorism. It became a better time to be a white-collar criminal, as the country was busy looking elsewhere. Paying a fine became simply the cost of doing business for major banks who made vastly more money than they paid in fines. It certainly was not a deterrent for future criminal activity.

The popular narrative that the banks and their executives buy themselves out of legal jams with campaign donations and lobbying is a compelling one. Certainly, the excess of money in politics has powerful implications.

However, the fact remains that during the previous crises, lobbyists and campaign influence was rampant, yet business executives involved in criminal behavior were successfully prosecuted. This idea cannot be dismissed entirely, since growth in American economic inequality and a loosening of campaign finance laws through Supreme Court rulings mean that the wealthy have even more political power. However, I find that this influence is more compelling in the arena of lobbying and lawmaking rather than in the criminal justice system. Certainly, the wealthy tend to fare better in criminal proceedings, but this is not due to campaign donations and political influence per se. Social connections as described in the cultural capture explanation can also be a factor, but those have also not meaningfully changed between crises. The wealthy and powerful in business and government have long been friends.

There are compelling reasons to believe it is prosecutorial discretion as influenced by the incentive structure and resources available for those prosecutors that provide the most direct explanation for why no high-level prosecutors were criminally prosecuted for the 2008 financial crisis. Specifically, prosecutors' decision-making was informed by internal Justice Department institutional factors (a recent preference for caution and a lack of resources) and the personal incentives faced by government prosecutors in the private sector. This will be a surprise to anyone pushing the popular narrative that the banks are simply too politically powerful. Certainly, there is a strong case to be made that they indeed are too powerful and "too big to fail," causing perverse economic incentives for them and making them harder to regulate. However, that is a policy question. I am seeking to answer a question that is fundamentally about law enforcement and about what are the best deterrents to white collar crime.

Ultimately, I seek to paint a picture of institutional incentives, rather than an explanation of decision-making for any one individual. The former prosecutors I interviewed and those quoted in the media generally say there was a lack of evidence for fraud or convincing a jury would be impossible. However, as savings and loan-era regulator Bill Black said in his Congressional testimony, if you do not investigate, you will not find.[22] Also, people are not always honest about their intentions, whether they realize it or not. Human psychology is complicated. People may not remember a long-ago decision-making process when asked about it years later, or they may not fully understand their own intentions even in the moment. Humans have a tendency to justify decisions they make in hindsight, especially based on who they perceive to be judging those decisions. In other words, when asked by a coworker at a private firm, an attorney may say they left government service because of the more comfortable life afforded by a private defense firm. However, when asked by an interviewer from a university, they may say it was because they believed in the mission of the private firm. Both of these answers may be true, or at least true at the time they are spoken. In short, humans are not always reliable sources of their own motivations and decision-making processes. Additionally, one government attorney could not have prosecuted a case alone. Therefore, there are group and institution-level dynamics at play as well, further complicating matters. Therefore, I chose to zoom out, looking at the incentive structures presented to these humans, rather than the individual humans themselves, following the general principle that most people will respond with a certain range of behaviors given the incentives to do so. This book outlines the incentives faced by a group and individuals at a particular moment in time. Incentives cannot predict or explain human behavior precisely, but they can tell us what these actors are being encouraged to decide. It is imperative that we pay attention to the institutional incentives to ensure human government actors are given the encouragement to behave in ways best for American society, rule of law and democracy. Institutions must be designed to incentivize this optimal behavior, acknowledging that government institutions are made up of human beings who will respond to the given incentives they face. Adherence to justice and the rule of law is one of the foundations of American government and it must be incentivized in our institutions if we do not want to see it slip away. Join me in this story and, when it's over, perhaps we can use our understanding to change our institutions so they can incentivize justice rather than injustice.

NOTES

1. Congressional Budget Office, *Report on the Troubled Asset Relief Program.*
2. United States FCIC, *The Financial Crisis Inquiry Report: Final Report of the National Commission on the Causes of the Financial and Economic Crisis in the United States*, p. 402.
3. In 2011 US dollars.
4. Treasury Department, *The Financial Crisis Response in Charts*, p. 2.
5. Official Hillary Clinton Twitter Account, January 17, 2016.
6. SIGTARP, *Special Inspector General Trouble Asset Relief Program Report to Congress*, p. 47.
7. McCarthy, *Americans' Confidence in Banks Still Languishing Below 30%.*
8. Sherter, *No Time: Feds Have Given Up Trying to Send Bankers to Jail.*
9. Irwin, *This Is a Complete List of Wall Street CEOs Prosecuted for Their Role in the Financial Crisis*
10. Keefe, *Why Corrupt Bankers Avoid Jail.*
11. Bloomberg News Editorial Board, *A Better Approach to Fighting White-Collar Crime.*
12. Greenspan, *Financial Times*, August 17, 2015.

13. Black, *Prepared Testimony—Examining Lending Discrimination Practices and Foreclosure Abuses.*

14. FBI, *Enron—Famous Cases & Criminals.*

15. Department of Justice, *Justice Department Announces Global Resolution of Criminal and Civil Investigations with Opioid Manufacturer Purdue Pharma and Civil Settlement with Members of the Sackler Family.*

16. Department of Justice, *Justice Department Announces Global Resolution of Criminal and Civil Investigations with Opioid Manufacturer Purdue Pharma and Civil Settlement with Members of the Sackler Family*; Mulvihill, *WATCH: Sackler Family Members Who Own Purdue Testify before Congress.*

17. Mulvihill, *WATCH: Sackler Family Members Who Own Purdue Testify before Congress.*

18. Department of Justice, *Justice Department Announces Global Resolution of Criminal and Civil Investigations with Opioid Manufacturer Purdue Pharma and Civil Settlement with Members of the Sackler Family*; Mulvihill, *WATCH: Sackler Family Members Who Own Purdue Testify before Congress.*

19. Kroft, *President Obama: The Economy, the Congress, the Future.*

20. Black interview.

21. Moon interview.

22. Black, *Prepared Testimony—Examining Lending Discrimination Practices and Foreclosure Abuses.*

Chapter 1

A Summary of the 2008 Crisis

In the years since the financial crisis of 2008, many narratives have been written to tell its story. The following is by no means the only or even the most interesting way to do so. For an in-depth discussion, there is Congress' Financial Crisis Inquiry Commission Report, and for entertainment, the movie version of Michael Lewis's *The Big Short*, utilizing Hollywood stars and a stew made from rotting fish by celebrity chef Anthony Bourdain.[1] Without the massive resources of Congress or the glamour of celebrities, the following gives the reader a basic background.

Banks used to want to know that a borrower could repay a mortgage loan before they made it. It was a huge investment and risk to lend out so much money to an average citizen. Therefore, these banks had an incentive to be careful when assessing whether a borrower was likely to repay the loan. Since the New Deal era, the government has sought to support these banks in their effort to make mortgage loans. For example, the Federal Housing Act of 1934 created the Federal Housing Administration (FHA) to provide affordable mortgage insurance to facilitate lending. With mortgage insurance, the lender could feel confident that they would not be left with a massive loss in the event a borrower could not repay, and the FHA is funded with the income from insurance premiums paid by mortgage borrowers. A major part of the push to support mortgage lending was the fact that two million construction workers had lost their jobs during the economic crisis. To reemploy these workers and stimulate the home buying and renovating industry, the New Deal sought to encourage homeownership in a country where nine out of 10 households were renters. Previously, banks made borrowing difficult for the average person, seeing them as too great a risk. They would loan only up to 50 percent of the property's value and payments were due within three to five years, as opposed to the 80 percent and 30-year mortgage loan that became standard later.[2]

A 1938 law created the Federal National Mortgage Association, commonly known as Fannie Mae. It was a quasi-government organization called a government-sponsored enterprise (GSE) that was created by an act of Congress, but privately held with a market-based purpose. Fannie Mae purchased home loans made by banks in exchange for cash that they could use to make more loans, allowing more people to buy or refinance homes. It then held the loans itself, receiving the monthly payments from the homeowners, or it bundled and sold the debts in a secondary market to investors. This bundle of loans sold off in shares to investors looking to receive reliable returns on their investment is known as a mortgage-backed security (MBS).[3] Additional government corporations known as Freddie Mac and Ginnie Mae were later created to further facilitate home lending. Later, government policies and rhetoric, especially in the 1990s and early 2000s sought to promote homeownership for as many Americans as possible, easing lending restrictions for these loans purchase by the GSEs in the process.[4] For example, President Bill Clinton announced an initiative in 1995 to push homeownership rates to 67.5 percent of families by the year 2000 and George W. Bush introduced a program that waved the already modest 3 percent down payment for first time homebuyers with FHA-insured mortgages.[5]

MBSs became an increasingly popular investment tool in the last few decades of the twentieth century at around the same time the investment banking industry began to hunger for higher payouts. As William D. Cohan writes in *Why Wall Street Matters*, beginning in 1970, investment banks began to change from partnerships to public corporations. As partnerships, they operated on funding from a privately owned pool of money belonging to these owners, who were accordingly risk averse in their investment strategies. However, as corporations, they could borrow money from the public markets and became more willing to gamble. Additionally, a system of bonuses heightened the risk-taking incentive. Business school and other academic stars began realizing Wall Street investment banks had become an attractive career choice, with the ability to make massive sums of money.[6] A man who did not come from academia, but worked his way up from the mailroom at Salomon Brothers, Lew Ranieri, is often credited with creating the so-called private label MBS in the late 1970s. With a private label MBS, investment banks could buy loan pools and sell off pieces of that pool to their investors. Both the banks originating the loans and the investment banks packaging and selling them made a lot of money in the form of fees for these transactions. Investors got a safe, reliable yield higher than the traditionally safe investment bond—the municipal bond. MBS paid out higher rates and were thought to be safe since the chances that a significant number of mortgage loans in any one pool would default were thought to be miniscule.[7] It seemed like a win for everyone. Investments based on mortgages had been considered among the safest, as long as the underlying mortgages were given to people who could afford them. Indeed, the major ratings agencies blessed most of them with AAA ratings, which is the highest rating possible and the same as a U.S. Treasury bond.[8] At the same time, 30 years of government deregulation loosened the finance industry from the grasp of government rules, so increasingly risky and complicated financial products were created around debt markets.[9]

Mortgage-based investments theoretically had safeguards built in, such as geographic diversity, bond insurance and higher-risk-higher-reward slices or "tranches" of the mortgage bond that would take losses first.[10] The investors in these tranches would be paid after those above them, making it more likely for them to lose money if any of the homeowners in the mortgage pool defaulted on their payments, but giving them a higher payout if all homeowners paid their mortgages reliably. These riskier tranches would sometimes get repackaged themselves into pools of pools, called Collateralized Debt Obligations or CDOs. Figure 1.1 shows the Congressional Financial Crisis Inquiry Commission's infographic created to educate the public and lawmakers on this complex process.

MBS were attractive investment products and banks soon faced more demand for them than they could deliver. They also invested in MBS products themselves, using massive amounts of "leverage," or borrowed money, to do so at times. Additionally, in the early years of the twenty-first century, after the dot-com bubble burst, the Federal Reserve lowered interest rates.[11] This also drove investors to look for ways to obtain higher returns, further fueling the demand for mortgage-based investment products. At this point, more loans were needed to package and sell. The investment banks began to encourage commercial banks originating the loans to be increasingly lenient with their lending standards to obtain more loans to package and sell to investors, as the demand for these investments outpaced the supply of so-called prime mortgages, which were considered the least likely to default.[12] Banks began easing down-payment requirements until many Americans began purchasing homes for no money down and with no documentation proving ability to repay. Credit score and income requirements dropped as well. These lower-standard loans were known as "subprime" and considered risky, as a borrower had less proven ability to repay and the terms of the loan were usually less favorable, such as with variable or higher interest rates. The GSEs would not buy them as investment products. With this ever-increasing demand for mortgages as investment products, even the riskier ones, home buying, refinancing and home equity lines of credit became more easily attainable, as banks were eager to lend. Figure 1.2 shows how subprime loans went from 8.3 percent of all new mortgages in 2003, to almost a quarter of new mortgages within three years.

Although much blame in the financial crisis story went to "greedy home buyers" taking on more than could afford, generally speaking, a borrower

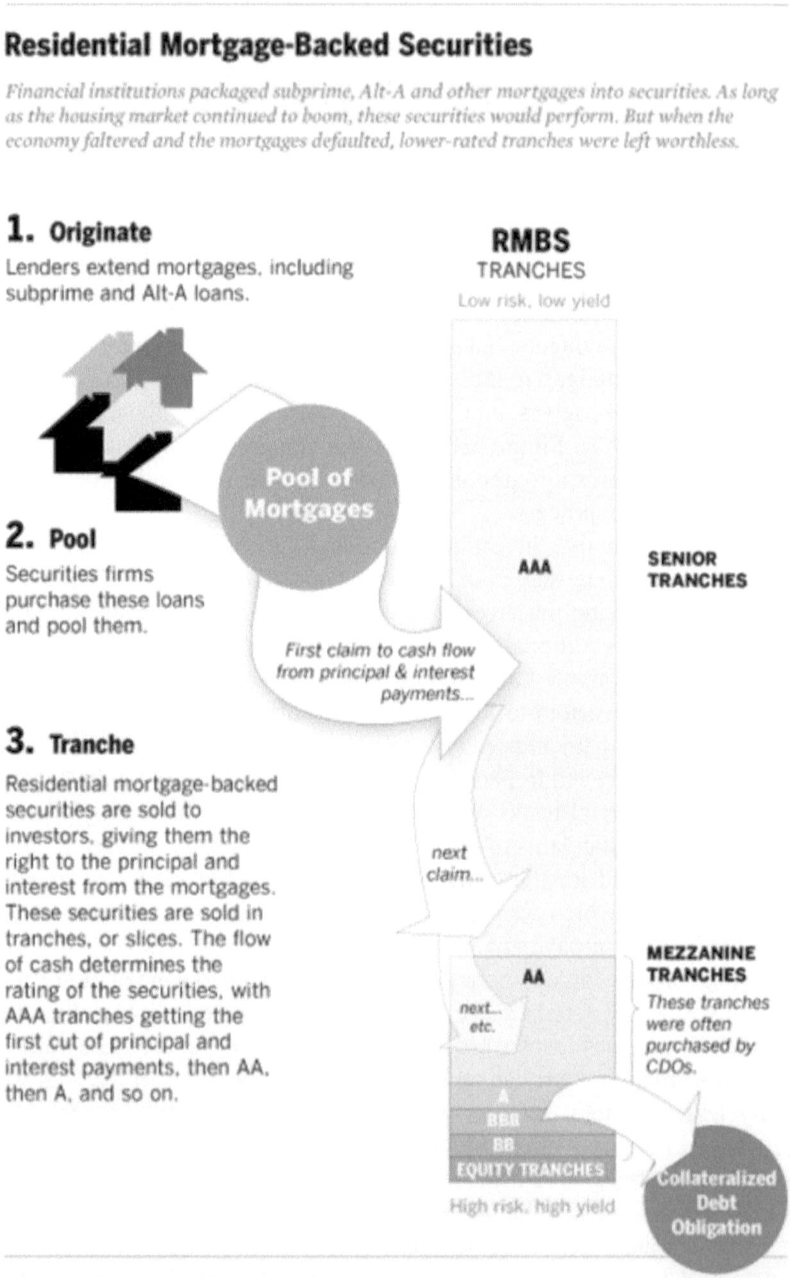

Figure 1.1 FCIC's Illustration on How an MBS Works.

Source: United States Financial Crisis Inquiry Commission, "The Financial Crisis Inquiry Report: Final Report of the National Commission on the Causes of the Financial and Economic Crisis in the United States—Resource Library," 2011, https://fcic.law.stanford.edu/resource/graphics.

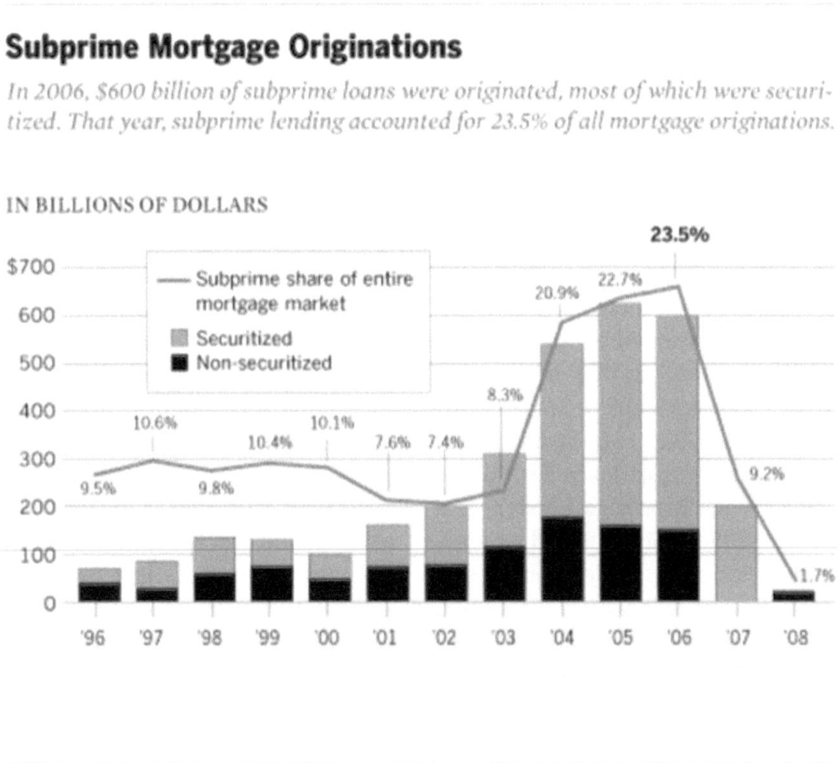

Figure 1.2 Subprime Mortgages Skyrocketed between 2003 and 2006.
Source: https://fcic.law.stanford.edu/resource/graphics.

is almost always at a disadvantage when taking on a complicated financial burden, such as a home loan. Most people don't fully understand the terms, fees and conditions to the extent the bankers do, particularly as mortgage products grew in complexity. This could lead a consumer to agree to loan terms that are ultimately not in their best interest. Perhaps they would have taken this risk even with full information, especially with the idea that after an initial two-year "teaser" or low rate expired they could simply sell or refinance. But perhaps they would not have taken on a mortgage that was more expensive than they could afford if given all relevant information. The incentive structure for the banks were in favor of pushing them into these loans. Additionally, an important but often ignored part of the story is the racial component. Racist government policies known as redlining had prevented Americans of color from buying homes in what were deemed "high-risk" (read as minority-dominated) neighborhoods, and racist homeowner covenants prevented them from living elsewhere. Civil rights reforms from the 1960s and 1970s had abolished many of these racist policies, but home buying was still difficult for minority populations as many lacked the generational wealth accumulated by whites, dealt with unconscious prejudices, had fewer stable job opportunities, etc. By the 1990s, minorities were disproportionately offered what activists described as "predatory" or subprime loans instead.[13] Dymski, Hernandez and Mohanty argue that economists tend to ignore racist policies and predatory lending. Even before the subprime crisis, black and Latino borrowers were twice as likely as whites to receive subprime loans, partly due to the lack of available regulated mortgage bankers in their neighborhoods.[14] "If minority neighborhoods and applicants were so systematically unworthy of housing credit at the same rates as other areas and applicants, how did they become so systematically included with the advent of the subprime loan?"[15] Some borrowers who could have qualified for lower-cost loans—like FHA-insured or Veteran's Administration loans—were pushed into riskier loans for this reason. For example, in December 2006, Countrywide Mortgage Lenders LLC settled with then New York Attorney General Elliot Spitzer to end a two-year investigation into allegations that the lender was specifically pushing black and Latino borrowers into high-cost loans. Countrywide agreed to compensate these borrowers, improve internal fair lending policies, and pay three million dollars for an independently run mortgage education program targeting minority communities.[16],[17]

Lenders were incentivized to make these higher-interest loans, as they earned millions of dollars in fees originating them, while passing on the risk by selling these loans to investment banks, who then packaged and sold them to investors. Countrywide is a prime example of an originator bank becoming a "fee machine."[18] In 2006, it had revenue of $11.4 billion and pretax income of $4.3 billion.

> When borrowers close on their loans, they pay fees for flood and tax certifications, appraisals, document preparation, even charges associated with e-mailing documents or using FedEx to send or receive paperwork, according to Countrywide documents. It's a big business: During the last 12 months, Countrywide did 3.5 million flood certifications, conducted 10.8 million credit checks and 1.3 million appraisals, its filings show.[19]

Countrywide and its commissioned employees were incentivized to push riskier, high-cost loans on borrowers because they garnered more in fees. During the peak years of subprime lending, these borrowers were often given adjustable-rate mortgages (ARMs), as compared to prime borrowers, who typically receive fixed-rate mortgages, with a steady interest rate locked in for the life of the loan. These ARMs often had low interest rates to start, which then skyrocketed after two or three years, when the introductory "teaser" rate period expired. Other subprime loans featured negative amortization, meaning the principal balance grew over time. These loans were complicated and risky, but during the exuberance of the housing bubble, all that seemed to matter was getting easily getting a borrower a loan. Even if the borrower could understand that the interest rate would rise in a few years, the general wisdom was that a borrower could simply sell or refinance at that point. There was no consideration that the housing market would crash, leaving buyers with no ability to sell and with an unaffordable mortgage. Although Countrywide was certainly not the only subprime lender fueling the bubble and preying on borrowers, "In terms of being unresponsive to what was happening, to sticking it out the longest, and continuing to justify the garbage they were selling, Countrywide was the worst lender," Ira Rheingold, executive director of the National Association of Consumer Advocates told the *New York Times* in 2007. "And anytime states tried to pass responsible lending laws, Countrywide was fighting it tooth and nail."[20]

Eventually the housing market became saturated, and prices began to drop due to excessive supply. It's hard to forget the sight of new homes being constructed seemingly everywhere in the middle of the century's first decade. At the same time, government regulators increased interest rates again, causing a shocking and unaffordable increase in monthly mortgage payments for many Americans and an inability to sell off their now unaffordable homes. Many homes were "underwater," that is, worth less than the balance of the mortgage loan owed on the house. Housing values continued to plummet in a positive feedback loop. Loan defaults and foreclosures began en masse.[21]

The three major rating agencies, Standard & Poor's Global Ratings, Fitch Ratings Inc., and Moody's Investor Services Inc.—which were paid by the investment banks to rate their products in a perversely incentivized manner—initially gave most of these mortgage-backed investments AAA ratings, the safest score possible. However, millions of homeowners began to default on their loans all at once, and the investment products that relied on these loans for their periodic payments began to drop in value. This decline in value then impacted the more complicated variations of the MBS, like CDOs, as well as products called synthetic CDOs, and CDOs squared, which were only remotely based on any original mortgage loans but were still impacted by the price crashes. The massive losses reverberated throughout the financial system, as all major investors seem to have a piece of some mortgage investment product or another. The rating agencies dropped the AAA ratings on many investments, as defaults continued to mount, eventually lowering many of them to junk status and furthering the panic, as investment banks and many other wealthy investors saw much of the value of their holdings disappear into thin air. A 2011 congressional pointed to the mass downgrade by rating agencies as the lynchpin of the financial crisis.[22]

Like a massive and dangerous game of musical chairs, everyone wanted to sell their mortgage-backed investment products before they were worthless, further pushing down their value. Some investment banks, like Goldman Sachs, had also invested in credit default swaps (CDS)—essentially insurance contracts or hedges on the mortgage products. CDS were part of a largely unregulated and opaque corner of the finance world known as "derivatives."[23] (In a stroke of intelligent foresight or evil genius, depending on your point of view, Goldman had even taken out CDS contracts on the very investments they sold to their own customers.) When the music finally stopped in 2007, some banks were in a better financial position than others. The situation had devolved into an economists' nightmare; a lack of something ephemeral but omnipotent and essential for the very functioning of the American economic system—trust.[24] Investment banks stopped lending to each other, which was an essential source of funding for daily operations. Everyone was in panic and self-protection mode. Despite government injections of cash and consolidations of banks, this this credit seizure eventually rippled into all corners of the economy, such as borrowing for daily operations and expansions in businesses thought to be far beyond the reach of Wall Street. Companies laid off workers, Americans had less money to spend, so companies had less cash to pay employees, and on and on.[25]

In 2008, finance officials in the George W. Bush administration took extensive measures to stabilize the economy, focusing on the banks. The government aided J.P. Morgan financially in buying the barely breathing body of investment bank, Bear Stearns Companies Inc., in March 2008, while letting Lehman Brothers Holdings Inc. die and declare bankruptcy in September 2008. Not wanting to be responsible for helping all of the banks like they had done with J.P. Morgan and Bear Stearns, but also not wanting to see a domino effect of bankruptcies beyond Lehman, government regulators encouraged other mergers designed to rescue banks teetering on the brink of failure, including Bank of America Corporation's purchase of Countrywide Mortgage and Merrill Lynch.[26] American International Group Inc., known as AIG, was by far the largest issuer of CDS policies, and when many of these insurance payouts on failing mortgage investments all came due at once, with much of the pressure to pay out coming from Goldman Sachs, the company faced insolvency. The insurance company received a $122 billion bailout loan from the federal government. Fannie Mae and Freddie Mac became insolvent, too, and as already quasi-government agencies, they were taken over by the government entirely in 2008.[27] Congress passed a $700 billion bailout package known as the Troubled Asset Relief Program designed to provide available cash (known as liquidity) to the major banks so they could continue operating, hoping to stop the reverberation throughout the economy. President Obama took office in 2009 and focused on further stabilizing the economy with a massive stimulus package. In 2010, he also oversaw the passage of the Dodd-Frank Financial Reform act to, in-theory, prevent in the future some of the problems that occurred during the crisis. Once the dust settled, some questioned whether the disaster was entirely the fault of overexuberance for mortgage products, or had some illegal activity also taken place. In cases where fraud had been initially suspected, investigations went only so far. The government sought settlement agreements. Banks paid billions of dollars in fines—which could be used for tax write offs and was paid by the company rather than by any person—for their actions during the crisis. Yet, no executive responsible for what may have been illegal, fraudulent behavior contributing to the systemic damage done to the economy and millions of Americans was criminally prosecuted. The public has since wondered if anyone deserved to go to jail. Certainly, if any illegal activity did occur, there remains little disincentive for it to happen again.

NOTES

1. Galarza, "Watch Anthony Bourdain Compare Fish to Finance in 'The Big Short.'"
2. Department of Housing and Urban Development. Federal Housing Administration, "About Us."
3. Fannie Mae, "About Us."
4. FCIC Report, p. 41.
5. FCIC Report, p. 41.
6. Cohan, *Why Wall Street Matters,* pp. 79–80, 87
7. FINRA, *Mortgage-Backed Securities,* Cohan, pp. 88–89.
8. Ashcraft, Goldsmith-Pinkham, and Vickery, *MBS Ratings and the Mortgage Credit Boom*, p. 1.
9. FCIC Report.
10. United States Financial Crisis Inquiry Commission Resource Library.
11. FCIC Report, p. 60.
12. FCIC Report.
13. Dymski, Hernandez, and Mohanty, *Race, Power, and the Subprime/Foreclosure Crisis: A Mesoanalysis*, pp. 19, 25.
14. Dymski, Hernandez, and Mohanty, *Race, Power, and the Subprime/Foreclosure Crisis: A Mesoanalysis*, pp. 6–8.
15. Dymski, Hernandez, and Mohanty, *Race, Power, and the Subprime/Foreclosure Crisis: A Mesoanalysis*, p. 16.
16. New York State Attorney General, *Countrywide Agrees to New Measures to Combat Racial and Ethnic Disparities in Mortgage Loan Pricing*, December 5, 2006.
17. This is in no way an adequate treatment of the racialized components of the financial crisis. There are mountains of inequity built into the American financial system. Other works have already better addressed these inequities and I hope in

future works to address them further. A Google search of “Racial injustice in home lending” produces more than 7.3 million hits, including countless news articles, research papers and books. For example, Heather McGee’s *The Sum of Us,* has a terrific overview on the subject.

18. Morgensen, *Inside the Countrywide Lending Spree.*
19. Morgensen, *Inside the Countrywide Lending Spree.*
20. Morgensen, *Inside the Countrywide Lending Spree.*
21. FCIC Report.
22. Younglai, Rachelle, and Lynch. *Credit Rating Agencies Triggered Financial Crisis, U.S. Congressional Report Finds.*
23. FCIC Report.
24. FCIC Report.
25. FCIC Report.
26. Flaherty, *BofA CEO Says Government Pressured Bank to Buy Merrill Lynch.*
27. New York Fed.

Chapter 2

Blue Sky and Beyond

Over exuberance or investment mistakes are not the same as conspiracy or fraud. Both may be undesirable and contribute to a massive financial crisis, but the former are policy problems and the latter are questions of law enforcement. At an asset-backed securities industry event in Las Vegas, I heard insiders compare people who sell mortgage-based investment products to car salesmen. Anyone who has gone through the often-painful car-buying process knows that a buyer must be prepared. The same goes for buying a home or investing in mortgage-backed financial products. The latter are savvy professionals, working as full-time fund managers or something similar. Even so, there is still an information imbalance between someone selling a product and the person buying it. Regardless of the product, there are laws governing the difference between an enthusiastic salesman and an outright liar. Leaving our car salesman analogy behind, let's take quick journey through the history of financial fraud laws in the United States.

Although financial frauds extend far back in human history, government regulation of them are relatively newer in the United States. For example, since fraud and manipulation of the stock market was mostly a battle between the wealthy, government regulation was seen as unnecessary. This attitude aligned with a general laissez-faire economic approach to regulation throughout much of the country's history. However, after World War I increasing numbers of average Americans began investing.[1] States responded to complaints of fraud from investors by passing "Blue Sky" laws, known as such because if they were not enacted, "financial pirates" would sell investors "everything but the blue sky."[2]

However, enforcement of these laws varied and faced some fundamental challenges. Government officials were inexperienced and underfunded in their efforts. Even more significantly, fraudsters could simply pay off a complaining witness, and the government would be forced to drop the case for lack of evidence. The Investment Bankers Association told its members in 1915 that they could evade Blue Sky laws simply by operating across state lines.[3] States competed with each other to attract investors and they were reluctant to adopt stringent regulations that might discourage business. For example, New York's Martin Act, passed in 1921, had potential to be an effective Blue Sky law, as much of the nation's securities were originated in New York. However, New York also did not want to diminish its role as an investment hub, and lawmakers feared a too powerful law would encourage corruption of officials enforcing the law.[4] Additionally, stocks listed on the New York Stock Exchange were exempted from Blue Sky laws. These early attempts at protecting investors still left many opportunities for fraud.[5]

In the 1920s, demand for securities continued to increase. Unscrupulous securities dealers created fake stocks to meet this demand. Other than promising quick riches, dealers gave little information when selling stocks to eager buyers, making fraudulent sales quite easy. Lawmakers estimated that approximately half the securities issued in that period were "worthless."[6] Several bills were proposed in Congress to rectify the situation, but the Roaring Twenties' exuberant mood made them unpopular until people began to lose money. In 1922, Illinois Congressman Edward Dennison proposed a law that would make it a crime to use the U.S. mail system to commit financial fraud, closing a major loophole in the Blue Sky laws. However, the Coolidge and Hoover administrations were committed to keeping financial regulation at the state level.[7]

In the exuberance of the 1920s, many people bought stock "on margin," or by borrowing money. Typically, people put down only 10 percent of their own money, borrowing the rest, with the stock as collateral. Beginning in September 1929, the market began to flag. On October 28, 1929, known as Black Monday, the Dow Jones Industrial Average declined 13 percent in one day.[8] By 1932, the Dow Jones Industrial Average was 89 percent below its pre-crash peak (it did not recover to its previous height until November 1954) and approximately 25 percent of Americans were unemployed.[9],[10] As panicked Americans flooded banks with requests for account withdrawals that they could not accommodate all at once, President Herbert Hoover called for banks to enforce their internal regulations.[11] Without enough cash to honor deposits, thousands of banks began to close and many Americans lost their life savings.[12] In January 1932, a newly passed law created the Reconstruction Finance Corporation to help banks and railroads that were illiquid (without ready cash) but had collateral to borrow against. This quasi-public agency could provide discount loans to struggling financial institutions, and through them, other businesses. It was expanded in July to include state and local governments as well.[13]

Amid rumors of "bear raiders" seeking to undermine stabilization efforts, the Senate Banking and Currency Committee began in March 1932 to investigate stock market practices, in. At first, bankers stonewalled the process, evading questions and failing to produce internal documents. The Committee made little progress until the Republican Chairman, Peter Norbeck, hired a New York deputy district attorney and skilled investigator, Ferdinand Pecora, as chief counsel.[14] Pecora and his staff subpoenaed and examined thousands of internal bank documents. His memory for detail and skillful questioning elicited scandalous admissions from bank executives called to testify, including chairman of National City Bank, Charles Mitchell. The committee chose Mitchell to testify because of the role of National City (predecessor of today's Citibank) as one of the country's largest banks and "its recognized leadership in the orgy of speculation which led to the business collapse."[15] Although Mitchell hadn't broken any laws, he outraged a suffering public with admission of his more than $1.2 million salary in 1929 and sale of massive amounts of company stock to a relative at a loss to avoid paying income taxes.[16] The commercial bank also convinced many of their customers to purchase risky stock sold by its investment affiliate. Many average Americans did so unquestioningly on the advice of bank professionals and lost their entire life savings, while executives enriched themselves behind closed doors. The airing of these practices during Pecora's questioning led to Mitchell's resignation in disgrace only days after the executive basked in the glow of wealth and power.[17]

The so-called Pecora investigation culminated in a 400-page report in June 1934, highlighting the finance industry's legal and ethical transgressions (presaging the Financial Crisis Inquiry Commission Report 77 years later.) It helped turn popular sentiment against laissez-faire capitalism and "banksters," like Mitchell, who had been celebrities only a few years prior. Pecora's dogged investigations and these public hearings paved the way for Franklin D. Roosevelt and the new Democratic party majority in Congress to pass the Securities Act of 1933, the Securities Exchange Act of 1934—which created the Securities and Exchange Commission to regulate the industry—and the Banking Act of 1933, also known as Glass-Steagall, which separated investment banking from commercial banking and created deposit insurance.[18] Roosevelt and Congress also passed the Trust Indenture Act of 1939 to regulate debt securities, the Investment Company Act of 1940 to minimize conflicts of interest in companies that both trade in and issue their own securities, and the Investment Advisers Act of 1940 to regulate those giving investment advice. A key provision of the Securities Act of 1933 was the registration statement, which required numerous disclosures to the federal government and a securities prospectus for buyers. Banks would have to provide all necessary and relevant information, without being misleading, or potentially face legal consequences. The law allowed civil and criminal penalties for failing to release a compliant statement or releasing one with false or misleading information.[19]

Perhaps most importantly for financial crime prosecution are the mail and wire fraud statutes. Mail fraud became a federal crime in the years just after the Civil War. In the antebellum period, extending all the way back to the colonial era, lotteries and other schemes were common sources of revenue for state and local governments. The practice came to the colonies from Europe. Many unscrupulous schemes reached people's homes through their mailboxes as well. An agent would send out mass-mailings advertising a variety of schemes promising some sort of monetary or material gift. People would send money, but nothing would arrive in return. In other cases, people would send in money and receive a package containing nothing but sawdust or fake money. The Postal Service would take unwarranted blame for this promised but undelivered gift. In 1872, Congress sought to protect the Postal Service by passing legislation to outlaw use of the mail to defraud the public in a scheme to obtain money. A revision to the law in 1909 effectively made it into a more general anti-fraud statute, rather than the narrower protective measure for the Post Office it once was.[20] Later in the twentieth century, a wire fraud statute was enacted for a similar purpose, outlawing the use of interstate telephone or electronic communication for this type of purpose.[21] Even the Racketeering Influenced Corrupt Organization (RICO) Act of 1970, originally intended to combat the Mafia, has been used to punish financial fraud, as has the savings and loan crisis-era Financial Institutions Reform, Recovery, and Enforcement Act (FIRREA), Dodd-Frank Wall Street Reform and Consumer Protection Act of 2010, and other statutes.

Fraud charges under most of these laws carry a five-year statute of limitations (except FIRREA), which was an issue commonly mentioned among those watching whether bankers would face any charges in the years after the 2008 crisis.[22] Using these and other laws, federal prosecutors have a variety of tools available and tremendous discretion about whom to charge with what. State prosecutors have their own set of laws as well. Prosecutors can also choose whether to bring criminal or civil charges, but only criminal cases can result in jail time. However, the challenge of any criminal prosecution is that it requires a higher standard proof of intent to break the law, rather than the lower standard for civil cases.

NOTES

1. Beattie, The Pioneers of Financial Fraud, Investopedia.
2. Keller, Introduction to Securities Acts.
3. Keller, Introduction to Securities Acts.
4. Keller, Introduction to Securities Acts.
5. Keller, Introduction to Securities Acts.

6. Keller, Introduction to Securities Acts.

7. Keller, Introduction to Securities Acts.

8. Richardson et al., "Stock Market Crash of 1929," *Federal Reserve History.*

9. United States Senate, Subcommittee on Senate Resolutions 84 and 234.

10. Richardson et al., "Stock Market Crash of 1929," *Federal Reserve History.*

11. United States Senate, Subcommittee on Senate Resolutions 84 and 234.

12. This is an extremely brief discussion of the Great Depression. See one of the myriad other texts for a full treatment of this crisis.

13. Gou et al., "Banking Acts of 1932,." *Federal Reserve History.*

14. For a fascinating biography of Pecora and his time on the committee, check out Perino, *The Hellhound of Wall Street.*

15. United States Senate, Subcommittee on Senate Resolutions 84 and 234.

16. United States Senate, Subcommittee on Senate Resolutions 84 and 234.

17. Perino, *The Hellhound of Wall Street.*

18. United States Senate, Subcommittee on Senate Resolutions 84 and 234.

The separation component was overturned in 1999 under the premise of financial modernization.

19. Keller, Introduction to Securities Acts, Securities Act of 1933, Section 10.

20. Abrams, "Uncovering the Legislative Histories of the Early Mail Fraud Uncovering the Legislative Histories of the Early Mail Fraud Statutes: The Origin of Federal Auxiliary Crimes Jurisdiction Statutes."

21. Justice.gov.

22. Dengel, "Second Circuit Rules that FIRREA's Ten-Year Statute of Limitations Applies Even When Banks Participate in the Fraud."

Chapter 3

Can a Company Be the Bad Guy?

Just as fraud is nothing new, neither is punishing people for disobeying society's rules. However, punishing corporations is a more recent and less intuitive strategy for law enforcement. Like many American institutions, the corporation was built upon British beginnings. In England, only the crown could grant a corporate charter to certain preferred entities, mostly municipal governments. In the new United States, the founders sought to democratize this process. Corporate charters granted by legislatures were at first given to form local governments, schools, and some charitable organizations. In the 1790s, economic enterprises start to become chartered as corporations as well. These charters—granted if one could successfully wield enough political influence—delineated capitalization limitations, length of existence, operation, function, and election by shareholders of directors. These corporations could enter into contracts and enforce them in a court of law. In order to further democratize these efforts, in the early nineteenth century states passed laws allowing for general corporation processes, rather than limiting incorporation to citizens with access.[1] A corporate charter also allowed limited liability, protecting shareholders from being held personally financially responsible for the corporation. In the decades after the passage of the Fourteenth Amendment, corporations successfully asserted that they were legal persons and therefore could sue over alleged violations of the Equal Protection Clause. However, the legal rights of shareholders were quite minimal beyond limited liability. There were few if any disclosure or reporting requirements, no accounting standards, and the rights of an average shareholder to sue directors was uncertain.[2]

By the turn of the twentieth century, corporate structures had often changed from few shareholders who also managed the company to many diffuse shareholders and professional managers separate from ownership.[3] Some American corporations had grown into massively powerful entities known as "trusts" that tended to wield oversize influence in political and economic processes. They often destroyed or purchased smaller competitors and monopolized markets. Workers had no choice but to accept low wages and dangerous working conditions, and customers were forced to pay artificially higher prices for their goods or services. In response, workers and others organized, forming unions and demanding reforms. In this so-called Progressive Era, the long, slow, hard-fought, and often non-linear process began to protect workers and consumers from corporate titans.

In terms of enforcing criminal laws, in 1909, the United States Supreme Court declared in *New York Central & Hudson River R. R. Co. v United States* that a corporation could form the necessary criminal intent vicariously through its officers, and therefore criminal charges could be brought against it for their illegal actions made on behalf of the company.[4] Federal courts have clarified over the ensuing years how and when a company may be held vicariously criminally liable for the actions of its employees. In 1970, a federal court ruled that a company may be held liable for criminal acts committed by a subsidiary, even if the illegal acts began before the merger or consolidation.[5] In 1972, a federal court said a company could be liable if a criminal act is committed by the employee in his or her general line of duty.[6] In 1989, this ruling was expanded to include acts committed on behalf of the company, even if they are against the company's general policies or compliance programs.[7] It is important to remember that intent must be shown to prove a criminal case. Proving a corporation had criminal intent may take various forms, including willful blindness to the crime(s); collective knowledge of criminal behavior within the firm, even if no single agent had enough knowledge to be convicted of the crime; active concealment of criminal behavior; and conspiracy to commit a crime.[8]

In the 1990s the idea of prosecuting a corporation received a boost in the form of an academic argument. A New York University professor, Ronald Goldstock, argued that prosecutors should focus on the criminogenic environment of corporations. Corporations, he maintained, are not simply collections of individuals; they also constitute environmental cultures, with incentive structures that may be conducive to a wide range of behaviors. If these behaviors are criminal, the corporation should be held criminally liable. This liability, he believed, should take a new form. Goldstock argued that prosecutors should attempt to reduce illegal behavior by targeting the organizational cultures encouraging this behavior. For example, in the case of certain types of crimes, like union corruption and mob influence, he argued that criminal prosecution of union leaders was not the best way to reduce criminality, and in fact may be counterproductive. Instead, a more productive remedy would be court-ordered trusteeships to instill more democratic practices. These structural changes of criminogenic organizations, potentially aided by self-monitoring, private auditing firms, public opinion, and other restructuring mechanisms required by government, could prove more useful than simply putting criminals in jail, he argued.[9]

Why look to prosecutors to change a criminogenic environment in a union, a city, or a bank? Goldstock argued that prosecutors are uniquely situated to have extensive knowledge of relevant laws and alternative options for enforcement, may have sole access to data from electronic surveillance, and possess the requisite discretion to negotiate for various reform measures in a settlement agreement (like the settlement agreements used extensively to deal with banks after the 2007 financial crisis).[10] Legal scholar Samuel Buell says the first modern corporate settlement agreement "famously" happened in 1994 with Prudential Securities Inc., whose defense counseled asked the Southern District of New York attorneys to defer indictment for securities fraud for a period of three years and drop the case at that time if the company successfully complied with the government's terms. The company also had to pay a $330 million fine and install a government-approved director. Three years later, a federal judge agreed to dismiss the case. The United States Attorney's office disclosed no information about why it chose to enter into this course of action and Prudential admitted no wrongdoing.[11] In 1996, the United States Attorney in Connecticut agreed to a non-prosecution settlement with accounting firm Arthur Andersen in connection with an investigation of a real estate company. The agreement called for a payment of $10 million and cooperation with the government in exchange for non-prosecution, but it disclosed no admission of wrongdoing by Andersen and no explanation by the prosecutors.[12] Andersen would not be so lucky next time.

Federal Judge Jed Rakoff—who served as chief of the business and securities fraud unit for the last two of his seven years (1973–1980) as an Assistant United States Attorney for the Southern District of New York—said this idea of "prosecutor as problem solver" was adopted by federal prosecutors in recent decades.[13] "It is the shift that has occurred, over the past thirty years or more, from focusing on prosecuting high-level individuals to focusing on prosecuting companies and other institutions," he wrote in a 2014 *New York Review of Books* article.[14] Charging companies and individuals need not be mutually exclusive practices, but experience shows that the Justice Department at times may prioritize one over the other. "It is true that prosecutors have brought criminal charges against companies for well over a hundred years, but until relatively recently, such prosecutions were the exception, and prosecutions of companies without simultaneous prosecutions of their managerial agents were even rarer," Rakoff said.[15] In an interview, he contrasted this trend with his tenure as division chief in the 1970s. "I used to say to my assistants . . . we used to think it was admission of defeat if we couldn't find the individuals," he said.[16] Pulitzer prize-winning investigative journalist Jesse Eisinger echoed Rakoff's assertion that the Southern District of New

York—a hub of white-collar criminal enforcement—historically focused on prosecuting individuals until recent decades. Additionally, the Transactional Records Access Clearinghouse—a research and data gathering organization at Syracuse University—reported in July 2015 that white collar prosecution of individuals was at a twenty-year low.[17]

NOTES

1. Fox, "What the Founding Fathers Really Thought about Corporations."
2. Hilt, "When did Ownership Separate from Control? Corporate Governance in the Early Nineteenth Century."
3. Berle and Means, The Modern Corporation and Private Property.
4. New York Central & Hudson River R. R. Co. v. United States 212 U.S. 481 1909. Skeptics maintained that as there was no corporate mind, the corporation was incapable of formulating the *mens rea* necessary for criminal prosecution.
5. United States v. Wilshire Oil Co. of Tex., 427 F.2d 969, 973–74 (10th Cir. 1970).
6. United States v. Hilton Hotels Corp. 467 F.2d 1000, 1004 (9th Cir. 1972).
7. United States v. Twentieth Century Fox Film Corp. 882 F.2d 656, 660 (2d Cit. 1989).
8. Poindexter, "Criminal and Civil Liability for Corporations, Officers and Directors."
9. Goldstock, 1992.
10. Goldstock, 1992.
11. Buell, "Why Do Prosecutors Say Anything? The Case of Corporate Crime," pp. 6, 7.
12. Buell, "Why Do Prosecutors Say Anything? The Case of Corporate Crime," p. 8.
13. Rakoff interview.
14. Rakoff, "Why Have No High-Level Executives Been Prosecuted in Connection with the Financial Crisis?"
15. Rakoff interview.
16. Rakoff interview.
17. Syracuse TRAC, accessed April 21, 2017.

Chapter 4

Justice Department Embarrassments

The secretive nature of federal prosecutors' decision-making process makes it difficult to give the American public a satisfying explanation as to why they declined to bring criminal charges against executives involved in the 2008 financial crisis. As outsiders, we can look at the incentive structure of the institutions in which they operate for some clues. Firstly, let us look at the history and structure of the Justice Department. The Judiciary Act of 1789 created the Office of the Attorney General, and George Washington appointed Edmund Jennings Randolph on September 26, 1789, as the first to hold that office. The same law also created the 94 United States Attorney's Offices. The president appoints—with Senate confirmation—the country's Attorney General, working at what is known as "main Justice" in Washington, as well as the United States Attorneys across the country. They are charged as the chief federal law enforcement official in their jurisdiction. After the Civil War, Congress passed a law including civil litigation in which the government is a party as part of the Attorney General's purview as well.[1]

The Reconstruction Era saw a flurry of activity for the Attorney General's office, particularly enforcing the new constitutional amendments and combating the Ku Klux Klan. To deal with this workload, in 1870 Congress created a Department of Justice (DOJ) to support the Attorney General. The Office of the Solicitor General was also created that year to represent the United States before the Supreme Court. In 1908, President Theodore Roosevelt created a group of special federal law enforcement agents known as the Bureau of Investigation. In 1935, this group became the Federal Bureau of Investigation and it is housed within the Department of Justice, reporting to the Attorney General. The FBI director is also a presidential appointee. The United States Attorney's Offices are also housed within the Justice Department, although how much independence they have can change with each administration. Reporting to the politically appointed United States Attorneys are a large staff of Assistant United States Attorneys who are hired as government employees, rather than appointed by elected officials.[2] The prosecutors at the Justice Department and the 94 U.S. Attorney's Offices in the United States are tasked with bringing criminal and civil cases for federal offenses. Additionally, only they can bring federal criminal charges, while other agencies can work on civil cases. (State and local governments have their own prosecutors as well.)

Prosecutors could not possibly (and probably should not) act on every violation of federal law. There are countless violations of myriad laws that occur every day in the United States. Therefore, prosecutors must choose which cases are worthy of their time and energy. A long-standing norm in the United States says that prosecutorial decisions should be made independently, without political influence, in order to uphold the rule of law. Overtly political prosecutions are the purview of non-democratic countries. Therefore, this norm mandates that the President not try to influence the Justice Department's prosecutorial decision-making. The strength of this norm has been tested by President Donald Trump's efforts to thwart it. President Trump has repeatedly publicly stated which actions he believes the Justice Department should take and has expressed his frustration at not being able to have more control over it. In fact, he said this to the *New York Times* in December 2017: "I have absolute right to do what I want to do with the Justice Department," he said, echoing claims by his supporters that as president he has the power to open or end an investigation. "But for purposes of hopefully thinking I'm going to be treated fairly, I've stayed uninvolved with this particular matter."[3] Despite his efforts, the inability for a President to command the Justice Department to charge his political enemies with crimes has remained intact. (Presidential influence will be addressed more in a later chapter.) Prosecutorial fairness and legal norms also necessitate a good deal of independence from Congressional control. To be sure, Congress asserts control over the federal bureaucracy through lawmaking, oversight, and budgeting powers, but it does not direct prosecutors on whom to charge and with what crime. Also, prosecutorial discretion is made without judicial review. While a case may reach a courtroom, which would be controlled by judicial oversight, charging decisions are not subject to a judge's approval. Judges will largely defer to prosecutorial discretion, except in clear cases in which motives based on race, religion or bad faith can be attributed to the prosecutor.[4] The logic of prosecutorial decision making is also not made public unless charges are filed. Even if a case reaches a courtroom, the prosecutors need not provide a public explanation of why they chose that case over others.[5] Considering that the vast majority of cases never reach a courtroom, as they are settled, and the decision-making process need not be disclosed, prosecutors operate with a great deal of independence from the three branches of government and operate outside of the public spotlight.

The secretiveness of this process can cause frustration for watchdogs, the media, academics, and the public. One way to better understand prosecutorial decision making is to examine the incentives and structures prosecutors face, as well as what provokes response and change from the institution as a whole. Public policy scholar Andrew B. Whitford argues that U.S. Attorneys are interested in maintaining their reputations and are protective against scrutiny of their decision-making process.[6] In the realm of white collar crime, they seem particularly responsive to outside pressures. For example, by the turn of the twenty-first century, businesses and their defense attorneys complained of an increasingly aggressive approach to prosecuting corporations and argued that the Justice Department had no coherent policy for charging corporations. In response, Deputy Attorney General Eric Holder, who would later become the Attorney General under President Obama, responded to these complaints with a memorandum, attempting to articulate a consistent and coherent policy.[7] The first in a series of memos that by 2008 would evolve into a virtual "get out of jail free" card for executives, was written in 1999 as a directive to prosecutors and was known as the "Holder Memo." It allowed for the possibility of taking into consideration the "collateral consequences" of charging a corporation with a crime, such as the punishment of innocent employees or other economic consequences. It also outlines the potential for using deferred- or non-prosecution agreements, in which the company agrees to make internal changes in exchange for the government withholding prosecution. Key factors the government would consider, according to the Holder memo, would include the company's willingness to cooperate, which controversially could include waiver of attorney client privilege and trade secrets.[8] All of these provisions would evolve through subsequent iterations of the memo and set the stage for the settlements of the 2008 crisis.

Legal scholar Samuel Buell argues that prosecutors disclose a surprising amount of information through these memos on prosecutorial decision-making rationale. They are detailed guides for prosecutors to follow, although they are not binding, and it is something they do not disclose for any other kind of defendant.[9] Why would the Department do this despite their usual secretive nature? Buell dismisses the idea that prosecutors speak publicly to influence jury pools or further their own careers. Attempting to influencing jury pools with the press may backfire more than help, and most federal prosecutors are not seeking the public notoriety that would be necessary to seek elected office later. More likely, they are seeking higher positions in the DOJ itself, a partnership at a "marquee" law firm—the kind that would have a lucrative white-collar defense practice—or a counsel position at a major corporation or investment firm.[10] Press coverage and name recognition may help in this quest, but it may not. What prosecutors most want, Buell says, is a resume with "big" prosecutions, "whether measured by complexity, size of settlement, importance of defendant, or seriousness and extent of wrongdoing."[11]

Although prosecutors want big cases, they don't want to risk a big loss. More than a big case, they want a big win. This can steer prosecutors to easy-to-win cases or settlements, rather than difficult cases against individuals. As for deciding whether to publicize their decision-making process, Buell argues prosecutors may want to prove to the public that they are tough but fair on corporations. They may also disclose these charging guidelines to mollify Congressmembers who are concerned they are too tough or too lenient on corporations, with more pressure on Main Justice than the United States Attorney's offices to respond to Congress for budget purposes or avoiding legislation. Prosecutors are also sensitive to the needs of corporations and the defense bar that represents them. White collar defense attorneys are treated with more respect and their clients are considered generally law-abiding citizens, as opposed to violent criminals. Therefore, federal prosecutors disclose more about their corporate charging procedures than they would for a mobster or drug dealer. Lastly, Buell considers that prosecutors may disclose more about corporate crime decision making to achieve a policy-making goal of deterring corporate crime in the future by giving firms guidance.[12]

ENRON-ERA BACKLASH

In the first five years of the twenty-first century, a series of accounting frauds designed to enrich executives at the expensive of shareholders and workers occurred and at some of the country's biggest companies, including Enron Corporation, WorldCom, Tyco International, HealthSouth Corporation, and Adelphia Communications Corp. With Enron being the most famous of these scandals that all came to light within a short period of time, I call this cluster of financial frauds the "Enron-era" crisis. In response to these frauds, the Justice Department criminally prosecuted systemically important executives like Enron's Chief Executive Officer Kenneth Lay and Chief Operating Officer Jeffrey Skilling, as well as Adelphia Cable's Rigas family.[13] Additionally, the Enron scandal included corporate prosecutions. The criminal prosecution of accounting giant Arthur Andersen in 2002 marked a turning point in the Justice Department's quest to change the criminogenic environment of companies. It was a relatively new concept to many who dealt with corporate fraud that executives could gain personal wealth at the expense of their own company. This lesson was not learned well enough from the savings and loan crisis, in which executives looted their own banks through creative accounting.[14] Certainly any misdeeds by executives from the Great Depression era had been long forgotten.

A 2010 American Bar Association (ABA) article praised the Enron prosecutions as a "watershed moment" for the Department in pursuing "greedy executives."[15] "Post-Enron, prosecutors became comfortable with casting a much broader net in the pursuit of fraud in the capital market," wrote Jacob Frenkel, a former federal prosecutor and a partner at the suburban Washington firm, Shulman, Rogers, Gandal, Pordy & Ecker in the ABA article "The Bush administration and opportunistic prosecutors saw the opportunity to bring high-profile, big-dollar cases against corporate leaders and public officials for how they conducted business."[16] The Justice Department also wanted to prosecute those who facilitated these accounting fraud scandals. And why shouldn't they? These executives cost many Americans significant sums of money; putting them in jail would show a prosecutor's toughness and would be a huge, public win for them personally. It was a difficult and ambitious approach, but it would backfire.

The Justice Department obtained a grand jury indictment in March 2002 of Arthur Andersen LLC, Enron's long-time auditor, charging the corporation with obstruction of justice for destroying documents to knowingly and willingly prevent an investigation.[17] Established in 1913, public accounting firm Andersen employed 85,000 people across 84 countries by the 1990s.[18] The Department alleged that Andersen began destroying documents related to special business entities that it helped Enron create—an integral part of what would later be recognized as Enron's accounting fraud—after the Securities and Exchange Commission started an investigation of the energy company. "As the indictment lays out, the destruction initiative began on or about October 10, 2001, as Andersen foresaw imminent government investigations and civil litigation. The destruction continued through the SEC's announcement that an investigation had been launched and only ended nearly one month later when the SEC officially served Andersen with a subpoena for Enron documents,"[19] said Deputy Attorney General Larry Thompson in a March 14, 2002 statement. A series of follow up press questions focused on the potential that this indictment would put Andersen out of business. Thompson, a Republican George W. Bush administration political appointee, replied:

> As I said in our statement, these are serious charges, and it shouldn't be a surprise to anyone that serious charges have serious consequences. And again, without talking about any particular matter, but just generally, *I think it would be unfortunate for our criminal justice system if any individual or any entity could say that he or she or it was too big or too important, so as it couldn't be indicted.*[20]

Thompson released an update to the Holder memo on January 20, 2003 guiding Department attorneys on charging corporations. This update came after three years of work by the Corporate Fraud Task Force and the Attorney General's Advisory Committee, created to deal with the Ernon-era cases. As a response to the Department's recent experiences, Thompson wrote:

> Too often business organizations, while purporting to cooperate with a Department investigation, in fact take steps to impede the quick and effective exposure of the complete scope of wrongdoing under investigation. The revisions make clear that such conduct should weigh in favor of a corporate prosecution. The revisions also address the efficacy of the corporate governance mechanisms in place within a corporation, to ensure that these measures are truly effective rather than mere paper programs.[21]

The general principle of the memo, Thompson wrote, was that "vigorous enforcement" of criminal laws against corporations benefits the public and law enforcement, "particularly in the area of white-collar crime," as it allows the government to be a force for positive change within a corporate culture.[22] However, this approach wound up causing serious embarrassment for the Department. The Department would be blamed for the destruction of an almost one-hundred-year-old, highly respected company and the loss of many innocent people's jobs. In 2002, Arthur Andersen lost most of its employees and clients after it was convicted of obstruction of justice. The firm could not operate without a trustworthy reputation, and a criminal conviction of this kind was undoubtedly poisonous. Thousands of blameless employees lost their jobs, shareholders were devastated, and vendors and others dependent on the corporation suffered. This could be seen as an unfortunate but perhaps necessary side effect of a successful prosecution. However, in 2005, the conviction was reversed by the Supreme Court on procedural grounds, making the company's destruction seem all for naught. The high court found that the district court, agreeing with the government's interpretation of the relevant law, failed to properly instruct the jury that it needed to find "consciousness of wrongdoing" when Andersen employees shredded documents. The Fifth Circuit court of appeals upheld the lower court's interpretation of the law that the "jury need not find any consciousness of wrongdoing to convict."[23] However, the Supreme Court wrote that simply shredding documents, even those related to a government investigation, should not have been enough to convict.[24] Whether the firm would have been convicted if the jury had received the stricter instructions as interpreted by the Supreme Court remains unknown. The Justice Department could have retried the case, but by that time Andersen was a shell of its former self, and the Department was blamed for destroying the company and prosecutorial overreach.[25,26,27]

Although the district court was responsible for the jury instructions, Supreme Court Chief Justice William Rehnquist wrote in the 2005 decision that *prosecutors* should have been more careful in their interpretation of the relevant federal laws, since the underlying act of shredding documents to hide them from the government is not "inherently malign," even though the shredding was done on Andersen's instructions. The corporate community and the press accepted Rehnquist's placement of blame and pounced on the Justice Department, which took this backlash seriously. "There's a big lobbying effort by corporations and the white-collar defense bar, saying Justice is abusing power," Eisinger said. "White collar lawyers say the Department of Justice is over-criminalizing business behavior and that there is prosecutorial abuse."[28] The Justice Department responded with more memos and a markedly more cautious approach to charging corporations. Somehow, charging individuals, which does not punish innocent others like charging companies can, was caught in the web of caution as well, despite Holder's and Thompson's earlier writings on the importance of individual culpability.

The ABA lobbied hard against the Holder and Thompson memos. Specifically, it objected to the provision seeking a waiver of attorney-client privilege for a corporation willing to cooperate in exchange for non-prosecution.[29] Acting Deputy Attorney General Robert McCallum sought to allay these concerns with an addendum to the Thompson memo that would require each U.S. Attorney's office to have a written waiver policy. However, as there was no requirement of consistency across offices, nor that the policies be made public, the policy did little to soothe the ABA's concerns. Senator Arlen Specter, a former prosecutor, introduced the Attorney-Client Privilege Protection Act of 2006, which provided increased protections for attorney-client privilege in corporate settlement negotiations. Also, Deputy Attorney General Paul McNulty issued a new memo to replace the Thompson version, which had replaced the Holder iteration. The McNulty memo changed the privilege waiver requirement policy to make it sought only if necessary. However, the edit did not bend entirely to the ABA and corporate pressure, as prosecutors could still maneuver around these restrictions by suggesting to a corporation that a waiver would benefit them even if not required.[30]

Despite the corporate and legislative pushback, and the Department's subsequent reforms, major embarrassments continued for Justice as the decade drew to a close. In 2007, a federal judge dismissed thirteen of the sixteen indictments in a tax shelter case against former employees of the accounting firm, KPMG (Klynveld Peat Marwick Goerdeler). Federal Judge Lewis A. Kaplan said the defendants' constitutional rights had been violated when prosecutors pressured KPMG not to pay their legal fees in exchange for not seeking an indictment against the company—a practice described in the Thompson memo. An appeals court later upheld the dismissals.[31] KPMG may have decided to cooperate with the government for fear that a criminal indictment against the company would mean a similar fate to that of Arthur Andersen only a few years prior. The Department again looked like it was abusing its power.

Another high-profile embarrassment for the Justice Department was a botched corruption case against a powerful Senator; Ted Stevens of Alaska.[32] Although the Stevens case did not involve the exact same type of corporate fraud as KPMG and Andersen, it was an extremely high-profile white-collar embarrassment for the Department, adding another nail in its bold prosecution coffin. In 2009, federal judge Emmet Sullivan overturned the Senator's conviction for failing to disclose thousands of dollars in gifts from an oil industry executive.[33] The Senator was indicted less than 100 days before the November 2008 election, in which he would be seeking reelection. Stevens was found guilty in October 2008,[34] just in time to lose his seat to Democratic Anchorage Mayor Mark Begich. Stevens had been the longest serving Republican in Senate history at the time.[35] Obviously, the loss attracted attention.

In December 2008, an FBI whistleblower said the government failed to disclose exculpatory evidence in Stevens's trial. Failing to turn over this kind of evidence to the defense is known as a "Brady violation" after the 1963 Supreme Court case Brady v. Maryland.[36] Judge Sullivan announced in 2009 that he had appointed a non-government attorney to investigate the Justice Department's misconduct in the Stevens case. Attorney General Holder declined to bring a new case against the Senator.[37] Stevens never served jail time, but the conviction obviously negatively influenced his reelection. The government lawyers were not legally held accountable for misconduct, which would have been highly unusual. However, the lead prosecutor on the Stevens case was found to have exercised "poor judgment" and left his government job. Two other prosecutors on the case were suspended (and later reinstated), and one committed suicide before the investigation was completed. Before the investigation ended, Stevens died a 2010 plane crash.[38]

Lastly, the unsuccessful prosecution of two mid-level Bear Stearns fund managers by Eastern District of New York attorneys in 2009 amounted to another major embarrassment for the Department; a final nail in this metaphorical coffin. The jury found the fund managers not guilty of fraud in November 2009, a verdict that William D. Cohan, a former Wall Street banker and author, wrote was "surprising—for its failure to conform with the *zeitgeist*," concluding that the prosecution "blew it." The response from the jury seems to confirm this notion. One juror told the *New York Times* that the jury felt the prosecution failed to make a good case.[39] After this loss, it was clear that the Justice Department had confirmed its own fears that financial crisis cases—based on proving fraud with intent, rather than overly zealous or unwise business decisions—were too difficult to prosecute successfully. Would the outcome have been different if more resources were allocated to the case?

NOTES

1. Justice.gov.
2. Justice.gov.
3. *New York Times*, December 28, 2017.
4. Whitford, 2002, p. 11.
5. Buell, p. 3.
6. Barkow, p. 313.
7. Lattman, "The Holder Memo and Its Progeny."
8. Holder memo.
9. Buell, p. 11.
10. Buell, p. 16.
11. Buell, p. 17.
12. Buell, pp. 18–27.
13. Crawford, Krysten, and Dunbar, "John Rigas Guilty of Conspiracy."
14. Black interview.
15. Persky,. "Aggressive Justice."
16. Persky,. "Aggressive Justice."
17. Department of Justice, News Conference—Arthur Andersen Indictment, March 14, 2002.
18. Brittanica.com, "Arthur Andersen."
19. Department of Justice, News Conference—Arthur Andersen Indictment.
20. Department of Justice, News Conference—Arthur Andersen Indictment; emphasis added.
21. Thompson Memo.
22. Thompson Memo.
23. Arthur Andersen LLC v. United States 544 US 696 (2005).
24. Arthur Andersen LLC v. United States 544 US 696 (2005).
25. Rakoff interview.
26. Mears, "Arthur Andersen Conviction Overturned."
27. Persky, "Aggressive Justice."
28. Eisinger interview.
29. Bishop, "The McNulty Memo—Continuing the Disappointment."
30. Bishop, "The McNulty Memo—Continuing the Disappointment."
31. Persky, "Aggressive Justice." United States v. Stein 07–3042-cr.
32. Savage, "2 Prosecutors in Case of Senator Ted Stevens Are Suspended."
33. CNN.com, "Sen. Ted Stevens' conviction set aside," U.S. v. Stevens, . April 7, 2009, No. 08-231 (D.D.C. Feb. 12, 2009).
34. Cary, "Recalling the Injustice Done to Sen. Ted Stevens."
35. Kane, "Sen. Ted Stevens Loses Reelection Bid."

36. Department of Justice, Office of Professional Responsibility, August 15, 2011.
37. CNN.com, "Sen. Ted Stevens' Conviction Set Aside."
38. Cary, "Recalling the Injustice Done to Sen. Ted Stevens."
39. DealBook, "Bear Stearns Trial: How the Scapegoats Escaped."

Chapter 5

Settling for Safety

Of the ninety-four U.S. Attorney's offices throughout the country, only some would have experience bringing major financial crime cases, as prosecutors deal with offenses within their geographical jurisdiction. Since Wall Street firms exist in New York City, and not Bangor, Maine, prosecutors working in New York City would naturally see more financial cases than in Bangor. John Moon served as a prosecutor at Main Justice in Washington from 1991 to 1993, during some of the savings and loan prosecutions. Some of the cases were brought in New England, and Moon was dispatched to help. "I brought some cases in Vermont and Maine. Assistant (United States) Attorneys would say, 'we don't even know how a bank works.' They bring lobster cases."[1] In other words, most federal prosecutors are not in New York or Washington and are focused on local cases. Even in New York or Washington, where financial crimes are the region's "lobster cases," the Obama-era prosecutors were still gun shy. The Justice Department maintains a 90 percent conviction rate for all criminal cases.[2] Conscious of their success record, they are unlikely to bring a case if they are not confident of victory.[3] Stephanos Bibas - a federal judge and former professor of law and criminology at the University of Pennsylvania Law School—wrote that instead of simply their perception of a suspect's guilt or innocence, prosecutors may be motivated by personal incentives. "They may be extremely risk-averse to protect their win-loss records, which further their employment prospects and political ambitions," Bibas wrote in a 2009 article. "Thus, they may press their own agendas at the expense of victims and the public."[4]

The series of high-profile embarrassments—especially taking the blame for a wholesale destruction of Arthur Andersen - created a chilling effect within the Department. "They got walloped in the press and they didn't want to lose again," said Neil Barofsky. This chilling effect means the Department might discourage risky prosecutions through resource allocation and management direction. Also, a career prosecutor who wants to move on to a more lucrative private practice after a few years will need to be more cautious.

Whereas being an assertive and tough prosecutor, especially in a high-profile case, used to be a good bet for a prosecutor's future career prospects, the very real possibility of blame for destroying a major company now added major weight to the strategy of playing it safe.

It is possible that a high-profile loss would not kill a career the prosecutor also enjoyed high-profile wins. For example, Andrew Weissman was a key player in the Andersen prosecution. However, he also was instrumental in the successful prosecution of Enron executives Kenneth Lay and Jeffrey Skilling, and earned a reputation as a tough prosecutor. Indeed, he was director of the Enron Task Force. He went on to positions as the General Counsel of the FBI and a prosecutor in Robert Mueller's Special Counsel's Office while it investigated Russian interference in the 2016 presidential election.[5] However, not all attorneys stay at the Department for as long as Weissman did, giving them less of an opportunity to make up for a high-profile loss. In fact, according to Harvard Law School, "a significant portion" of Assistant United States Attorneys spend five to seven years in the role before moving on to other work.[6]

The Department as a whole took on a more cautious tone. New attorneys in this era would be incentivized by the culture of caution and the Departmental reputation when thinking of their future careers, instead of taking a cue from the Andersen prosecutors. Ultimately, even a young prosecutor looking to repeat Weissman's aggressive approach, despite the risks and damaged Department reputation, may be standing alone, which falls far short of what is needed for a complicated government prosecution. Weissman had an aggressive task force behind him after all. Lacking adequate resources would be a serious disincentive to take on a complicated case. Additionally, he was already in a prominent position, not looking for a career-making or –breaking case. By 2010, the Department seemed to be firmly resigned to the safe road, relying entirely on settlement agreements with the major players involved in the 2008 financial crisis. Celesta Albonetti argues that prosecutors seek to minimize uncertainty when deciding whether to file charges, considering evidence, number of witnesses, defendant-victim relationship, gender, race, prior record, offense-type, victim-type and statutory severity.[7] Criminal procedural constraints, high caseloads, limited staffing and shared values and norms within the group of other prosecutors, judges and defense attorneys with whom prosecutors form working relationships are also important factors.[8] Additionally, the prosecutors' "self-concept" is as a lawyer, not as a law-enforcement official. Therefore, they will likely be cautious about embarrassing themselves by bringing a case lacking sufficient evidence, and less concerned with the practices of police investigative decision-making.[9]

Southern District of New York U.S. Attorney Preet Bharara said in an October 2010 speech at the American Bar Association entitled, "The Future of White Collar Enforcement," that although the Department was committed to its long-standing goals of aggressively pursuing financial fraud to ensure the safety and fairness of financial markets, "especially now, with the economy down, public frustration up, and epic frauds surfacing with increasing frequency," its attorneys were also conscious of collateral consequences. Prosecutors are aware, he emphasized, "that with our subpoena and grand jury power comes the power to injure individual lives and destroy corporate reputations. So, we must always take care to exercise our discretion with great care and an even hand."[10] In other words, be cautious. It is hard to imagine a prosecutor saying this just ten years earlier of Enron CEO Ken Lay, or a person accused of robbery, for that matter.

Bharara said he expected his Assistant U.S. Attorneys to be tough but fair, aggressive, creative, open-minded, and "supremely principled." He also said he was open to meeting with defense attorneys personally, if there were a complaint or appeal. However, despite private lawsuits and news articles piling up on the reality of toxic mortgage-backed products, Bharara spent much of the speech talking about insider trading; a seemingly tone-deaf choice. It is unclear to an outside observer why Bharara would focus on insider trading, rather than the hot topic of fraud. Based on the cases made from his office, an outsider could speculate that he was setting expectations and that insider trading cases might be easier to prosecute. A more straightforward case is easier to prove to a jury when trying to prove intent. Could it have been that fraud cases are more technically complicated, allowing for the used car salesman defense: the seller of mortgage bonds can plead that he was simply being an aggressive salesman? The remainder of the speech called on attorneys and companies to self-police and self-report issues, a strategy that has long proven to be unrealistic.[11,12] Bharara closed his speech by saying, perhaps a bit too idealistically given his office's lack of action on fraud cases:

> And so the truly great lawyer—motivated by conscience, guided by principle, and empowered by training—can serve as the greatest antidote against a creeping corporate corruption that has so sapped people's faith in our economic order. In the end, the good lawyer makes a living; the great lawyer makes a difference.[13]

Contrary to this sentiment, government lawyers relied increasingly on settlements known as deferred- and non-prosecution agreements. We know that no executives or companies from the 2008 financial crisis wound up facing criminal prosecution. However, when the initial announcement is made that the bank (or its executives) will not face prosecution as long as it "behaves" and it comes with a settlement amount reaching into the billions of dollars, the Justice Department looks tough. Media attention moves on before anyone checks whether the reforms were made. These agreements were attractive for an embattled and gun-shy Department, in that they required significantly less time, money and risk than criminal prosecutions, and could be presented as "wins" to the public. Known as "regulation by settlement," these agreements attempt to impose various reforms on banks in order to correct a criminogenic or unethical environment, but do so without the usual constraints applied to both regulation and litigation.[14] This change results from "increased emphasis on corporate (rather than individual) liability, skyrocketing monetary penalties, and the nearly exclusive imposition of those penalties via innovative legal instruments that facilitate out-of-court settlement," according to legal scholar Matthew Turk.[15] There is little or no judicial review, as there would be in litigation. For better or worse, the public comment process, interest group input, turf battles, congressional involvement and administrative agency actions can be avoided as well, unlike in legislation. Additionally, although settlements are made with single institutions at a time, they effectively establish widely applicable legal and policy standards.[16]

For example, J.P. Morgan's $13 billion settlement agreement may have sounded impressive to an angry public, but these fines, which punished blameless shareholders, employees, and vendors, and not necessarily the individuals responsible, permitted corporations to return to normal business operations and profit margins. Ostensibly, the financial services business continued as usual with extravagant bonuses paid top executives even after the crisis. In fact, multiple studies found that executive compensation structures incentivized excessive risk taking.[17] Also, in the midst of the crisis the banks consolidated, aggressively encouraged by government officials, becoming even larger. Indeed, they are now even more "too big to fail."[18] Mortgage securities attorney Isaac Gradman said the reliance on civil settlements creates a perverse incentive scenario for "Too Big to Fail" bank executives.

> They fall out in the wash when you factor in how much money the banks made from the entire enterprise of packaging and selling subprime mortgage-backed securities. The only real deterrence that I have found is the threat of criminal prosecution and the threat of personal disgorgement of profits from individuals. Otherwise there really is no deterrence for them not to perpetuate the exact same fraud in the future and just find more creative ways to do that. It's just the cost of doing business in that scenario.[19]

In other words, the settlements that the increasingly skittish Justice Department began to rely on made no meaningful law enforcement impact, and Department prosecutors' work environment changed. "They all become gun-shy about prosecuting individuals," Eisinger said. "They lose the skill set."[20]

Despite white collar prosecutions being at a twenty-year low, there was some activity in 2010 and 2011. The FBI's 2010–2011 crime report said that as the economy began to crater during the crisis, the

> FBI witnessed a steady rise in securities and commodities frauds as investors sought alternative investment opportunities . . . Since 2008, securities and commodities fraud investigations have increased by 52 percent, and the FBI currently has over 1,800 pending investigations. During this period, the losses associated with these types of schemes have increased to billions of dollars. The losses are associated with depreciative market value of businesses, reduced or nonexistent return on investments, and legal and investigative costs. The victims of securities and commodities frauds include individual investors, financial institutions, public and private companies, government entities, pension funds, and retirement funds.[21]

Perhaps the most famous among these cases are Bernard Madoff and Raj Rajaratnam. Madoff, who devised a massive Ponzi scheme, was turned in by his sons, pled guilty, and was sentenced to 150 years in prison in 2009, slightly before the spike in cases outlined by the data.[22] In 2011, Rajaratnam, an enormously wealthy insider trader, was undone by wire taps and sentenced to eleven years in prison. Reporting on the appeals court's ruling, the *New York Times*'s DealBook column applauded government prosecutors for their "aggressive" efforts on insider trading cases. "The ruling validates the aggressive tactics deployed by federal prosecutors in the government's sweeping investigation into insider trading on Wall Street, which has resulted in more than 70 convictions or guilty pleas since 2009."[23]

The FBI and its Financial Fraud Enforcement Task Force partners conducted "Operation Broken Trust," a sweep targeting companies and individuals for various securities fraud schemes occurring between August and December 2010, resulting in both civil and criminal cases.[24] On December 6, 2010, Attorney General Holder announced that the results of Operation Broken Trust were 343 criminal defendants—both individuals and corporations—including "more than 120,000 victims with losses attributable to alleged criminal activity of more than $8 billion."[25] According to the report, the most common types of securities and commodities fraud during this time period included Ponzi schemes, pyramid schemes, market manipulation schemes, confidence scams, foreign currency exchange fraud, precious metals fraud, broker embezzlement, and trading shares during prohibited hours. At the end of fiscal year 2011, the FBI reported 1,846 cases of securities and commodities fraud, 520 indictments, and 394 convictions. This is up from approximately 1,200 pending securities and commodities fraud cases in fiscal 2008.[26] This may seem like a flurry of activity and aggressive enforcement.

However, none of these cases were brought against individuals in charge of systemically important or "Too Big to Fail" institutions. In other words, those executives and companies that were charged criminally were less likely to have seemingly endless resources for defense and negotiation than those of the megabanks. Most importantly, it wasn't much of a deterrent for fraudulent but profitable acts by the leaders of megabanks in the future.

If the major cases highlighted in the FBI report included important sounding companies with big dollar values, it's hard to connect these dots to punishment of anyone systemically important in the 2008 financial crisis. The major examples in the FBI report include "Joseph Blimline, who orchestrated one of North Texas's largest oil and gas investment Ponzi schemes, defrauding 7,700 investors of over $485 million"; seven officials from A&O Entities of Richmond, Virginia, which sold shares in life insurance policies to mostly elderly investors in a $100 million Ponzi scheme; and New York-based Nicholas Cosmo, who ran a Ponzi scheme worth hundreds of millions of dollars.[27] These cases are likely important in their own right, but appear to be unrelated to the crisis at hand. What seems more closely related to the 2008 crisis, are mortgage fraud, financial institution fraud, and other crimes detailed in the report. The agency boasted 1,223 indictments and 1,082 convictions; $1.38 billion in restitutions; $116.3 million in fines; $15.7 million in seizures; and $7.33 million in forfeitures in fiscal year 2011. The FBI lists such mortgage fraud cases in this period as Luis Belevan and The Guardian Group, LLC of Phoenix; Howard Shmuckler, The Shmuckler Group of Washington, DC; and David Crisp of Sacramento.[28] However, Angelo Mozilo, co-founder of Countrywide Financial—responsible for billions of dollars in subprime mortgages and one of the biggest contributors to the financial crisis—learned in June 2016 that he would face neither a criminal nor a civil case from the Justice Department for mortgage fraud. (He settled with the Securities and Exchange Commission for $67.5 million, avoiding a civil trial, and the Justice Department simply dropped its criminal investigation.)[29] Mozilo has been an icon for public anger, while those men listed as case highlights in the FBI's report were comparably meaningless or irrelevant to the grander scheme of the 2008 crisis. How could these prosecutions possibly be a deterrence for men like Mozilo in the future?

Likely as a response to the immense public criticism the Department received for not prosecuting important executives, Assistant Attorney General Sally Quillian Yates issued her own memo on September 9, 2015, urging prosecutors to charge individuals.

> One of the most effective ways to combat corporate misconduct is by seeking accountability from the individuals who perpetrated the wrongdoing. Such accountability is important for several reasons: it deters future illegal activity,

> it incentivizes changes in corporate behavior, it ensures that the proper parties are held responsible for their actions, and it promotes the public's confidence in our justice system . . . There are, however, many substantial challenges unique to pursuing individuals for corporate misdeeds. In large corporations, where responsibility can be diffuse, and decisions are made at various levels, it can be difficult to determine if someone possessed the knowledge and criminal intent necessary to establish their guilt beyond a reasonable doubt. This is particularly true when determining the culpability of high-level executives, who may be insulated from the day-to-day activity in which the misconduct occurs. As a result, investigators often must reconstruct what happened based on a painstaking review of corporate documents, which can number in the millions, and which may be difficult to collect due to legal restrictions. These challenges make it all the more important that the Department fully leverage its resources to identify culpable individuals at all levels in corporate cases.[30]

This change of tune by a department that had been increasingly cautious on white collar crime again shows how sensitive the Department is to public and Congressional criticism, such as articulated by the 2011 Financial Crisis Inquiry Commission Report. It also articulates the importance of holding individuals accountable even though it is hard. Yates articulated the challenge of prosecuting any executive individually, especially in a megacorporation like an international investment bank, in which there are many layers of management to insulate those at the top. Instead of simply tapping phones, the government would have had to invest significantly more time and resources to build a case, following extensive paper trails and convincing lower-level employees to testify against their superiors. Yates wrote that her memo was the result of a working group that met to outline new and existing measures for the Justice Department to achieve these goals. It may have been too little, too late by 2015. Fraud statutes often have a five-year statute of limitations, but if the "fraud schemes affect a financial institution," the government may have 10 years to bring a case. Certainly, by 2018, time was up.[31]

These hard cases would have had true public value for their ability to remove the incentives for destructive financial fraud crimes and help restore public trust in the justice system. Yet, the incentive structure prosecutors faced within an evolving Justice Department that is sensitive to outside criticism made them all but impossible. It is reasonable for a government agency, funded by taxpayers and run by appointees chosen and monitored by democratically elected politicians, to be sensitive to outside criticism, at least to some extent. A democratic society necessitates accountability. However, the rule of law, which governs the way a fair and democratic society must conduct its affairs, necessitates that criminal prosecutions are based on an egalitarian application of the laws as much as possible rather than short-term reactions to a cautious Justice Department highly sensitive to outside opinions. To be sure, neither total accountability to affected groups, nor an entirely unbiased application of the laws is realistic. These two goals are both important and but also can be in conflict, not to mention law enforcement is conducted by human beings, not emotionless, selfless computers. Do prosecutors act on behalf of a nebulous notion of "the people"? Who are the people anyway? Corporate executives? Homeowners? An unclear notion of "the masses"? The truth is that prosecutors are lawyers, as well as human beings who have personal interests to consider, such as the ability to support themselves and their families. A better salary is a powerful incentive for even those most civic-minded, especially in an overwhelmingly expensive city like New York. These personal incentives are centered within an institutional incentive structure of a cautious Department that is receptive to outside criticism. Without resources and institutional support, as well as a personal disincentive to prosecute certain high-profile cases for fear of losing and ruining one's career, how could any difficult but systemically important case be made?

NOTES

1. Moon interview.
2. Department of Justice Executive Office for United States Attorneys, Fiscal Year 2010, Annual Statistical Report.
3. Ferguson-Gilbert, "It Is Not Whether You Win or Lose, It Is How You Play the Game: Is the Win-Loss Scorekeeping Mentality Doing Justice for Prosecutors?," pp. 289–290.
4. Bibas, 2009, p. 962.
5. New York University Law School, "Andrew Weissman Returns to NYU Law."
6. Baranouski, Ruttenberg, and Stein, 2014.
7. Albonetti, 1991
8. Stemen and Federick, 2012.
9. Katz, 1979, p. 442.
10. Department of Justice, Southern District of New York, "The Future of White Collar Enforcement: A Prosecutor's View Prepared Remarks of U.S. Attorney Preet Bharara New York City Bar Association," October 20, 2010.
11. Department of Justice, Southern District of New York "The Future of White Collar Enforcement: A Prosecutor's View Prepared Remarks of U.S. Attorney Preet Bharara New York City Bar Association."
12. Perino, *The Hellhound of Wall Street.*
13. Department of Justice, Southern District of New York, "The Future of White Collar Enforcement: A Prosecutor's View Prepared Remarks of U.S. Attorney Preet Bharara New York City Bar Association."
14. Turk, 2017, p. 2.
15. Turk, 2017, p. 2.
16. Turk, 2017, pp. 2, 3.

17. Bhagat, Sanjai, and Brian Bolton, "Financial Crisis and Bank Executive Incentive Compensation"; Bebchukt, Cohentt, and Spamann, "The Wages of Failure: Executive Compensation at Bear Stearns and Lehman 2000–2008."

18. Kwak, "Cultural Capture and the Financial Crisis."

19. Gradman interview.

20. Moon interview.

21. Federal Bureau of Investigation, Financial Crimes Report to the Public Fiscal Years 2010–2011.

22. Henriques, "Madoff Is Sentenced to 150 Years for Ponzi Scheme."

23. DealBook, "Rajaratnam Conviction Upheld by Appeals Court."

24. Federal Bureau of Investigation. Financial Crimes Report to the Public Fiscal Years 2010–2011,

25. Federal Bureau of Investigation, Financial Crimes Report to the Public Fiscal Years 2010–2011.

26. Federal Bureau of Investigation, Financial Crimes Report to the Public Fiscal Years 2010–2011.

27. Federal Bureau of Investigation, Financial Crimes Report to the Public Fiscal Years 2010–2011.

28. Federal Bureau of Investigation, Financial Crimes Report to the Public Fiscal Years 2010–2011.

29. Goldstein, "Angelo Mozilo Will Not Face Charges for Mortgage Fraud."

30. Yates memo, 2015.

31. https://www.justice.gov/archives/jm/criminal-resource-manual-968-defenses-statute-limitations.

Chapter 6

Case Studies from the Crisis

POTENTIAL EVIDENCE?

Even if prosecutors had the internal and external incentives to take on a difficult case, what reason do we have to think there was even a case to make? Or was it just a series of bad business decisions and irrational overinvestment in a bubble market? Some industry defenders, such as a former prosecutor and current white-collar defense attorney whom I interviewed anonymously, say financial professionals were simply overly exuberant. Why, then, did the government prosecute some much less influential mortgage industry people for crisis-related fraud? The federal government recognized there were bad actors in the financial crisis, but they were only to be found at smaller banks? The anonymous attorney said investment bankers packaging and selling the securitizations based on these loans likely suffered from misunderstanding, bad incentives, and poor forecasting, but not bad faith or criminality.[1] How is it that finance executives without powerful companies behind them knowingly committed fraud, while influential corporate executives simply misunderstood? The small fries are criminals, but the big wigs are gutsy investors? Or is it possible the government prosecuted easier cases and left the harder ones alone? Ultimately, if the government had conducted a thorough and wide-ranging investigation with a fully funded and staffed task force as had been the case with previous crises, the public may have a more satisfactory answer.

I will show in this chapter that there may have been evidence for criminality and bad faith at the highest levels of investment banking during the 2008 financial crisis. Without subpoena power or access to the Department's private files, of course I am unable to make a full argument of the evidence. I can only rely on what exists in the public record. However, I argue that this narrative collection of information provides adequate reason for the public to be skeptical about the Department's prosecutorial decision-making. Considering the systemic importance of this crisis and mistrust in government institutions it exacerbated, at the very least, a more thorough investigation and public report was warranted.

John Moon, a former white-collar federal prosecutor, pointed to the level of complexity as the difference between savings and loan-era prosecutions and the 2008 financial crisis. He said that the "bad acts" committed during the savings and loan era were simply easier to prove in a criminal case than those of the more recent crisis. "Everyone can understand giving out bad loans or phonying-up documents used to apply for the loan. Everyone can figure out that's bad behavior," Moon said of the earlier crisis.[2] In contrast, the 2008 crisis' mechanics would have been much harder to explain to a jury, Moon said. Indeed, a criminal case is hard to prove and even more so when the alleged crime is complicated. A criminal conviction requires proof that the actor intended to commit the fraudulent act or was willfully blind to it, and that the government had proven its case "beyond a reasonable doubt," rather than the lower civil standard of "preponderance of the evidence." In other words, a criminal conviction requires proof with almost total certainty, while a civil case only needs a likelihood of more than half. This is a challenge in itself, and rightly so. If the state wishes to deny a person of their constitutional right to liberty, it should have to meet a high burden. Still, criminal cases are made successfully in American courts of law every day. Does the fact that a case is more complicated mean it should not be tried? Doesn't this incentivize future financial criminals to just make sure their behavior is "too hard to explain to a jury"? Certainly, with highly intelligent people graduating from top colleges with degrees in mathematics, economics, or business flocking to work at investment banks because of the high pay, this should not be a problem.

The major difficulty in bringing a criminal fraud case is proving intent to defraud or the "knowingly" part. A person's knowledge or intent is hard to prove. Company officials can claim they could not foresee bad outcomes and were simply aggressively doing business with the best knowledge they had at the time. Unfortunately for the Justice Department, this is the defense used successfully in the Bear Stearns hedge fund manager fraud trial in 2009. This was a swing and a miss against mid-level managers. Certainly, this loss had a chilling effect on an institutionally cautious Department against going for any top executives. Additionally, federal court decisions have highlighted, if not increased this challenge. For example, in December 2010, a federal appeals court overturned the conviction of Prabhat Goyal, the former chief financial officer of Network Associates, on fifteen counts of securities fraud, making false filings with the Securities and Exchange Commission, and making false statements to the company's auditors, citing lack of sufficient proof of intent to defraud.[3] Additionally, finance executives would have the assistance of top white-collar defense attorneys, many with the benefit of previous experience working as a government prosecutor. I am certainly not arguing a criminal case against a high-level executive would be easy. As Acting United States Attorney General Sally Q. Yates said (quoted in an earlier chapter) corporate executives may be well insulated in a fraud scheme, but that is all the more reason to pursue them.

Increasingly extreme economic inequality and mistrust in the American justice system, as well as the following examples suggest that further efforts were warranted. I argue that more aggressive prosecutors with the right incentives and resources could have brought some effective cases or at least provided the public with the results of a deeper legal investigation. The American rule of law required some public efforts to hold finance executives accountable even if it was more difficult this time. Congressman Al Green, Democrat of Texas, summed up during an April 20, 2010 hearing on the Lehman bankruptcy the frustrations of the American public and many elected officials:

> How can this kind of thing . . . how can this go on and no one suffers some sort of criminal investigation to the extent that the public is aware of it? This is just amazing. When I read this information, I was thunderstruck. Because I couldn't believe that all of this information is available and we haven't seen anyone arrested. The public at some point has to see some sort of effort to bring to justice people who do this and that take advantage of so many others with these misleading and incorrect documents.[4]

CLAYTON HOLDINGS LLC

As a simplified and general description of the process, when investment banks want to create a mortgage-backed security for sale to investors, they need to purchase thousands of mortgage loans for each of these investment products. Investment banks buy them from commercial banks—known as the originators—that made the loans to people so they could buy a house. To be sure that these loans were likely to be repaid, the investment banks could examine the documentation behind the loans to ensure they were made to borrowers likely to make their loan payment each month. However, the purchasers—known as the securitizers—find it impractical to examine the entire file of paperwork for each loan, so they would take a sample to examine instead. A sample could be between 30 percent of the loan pool to as little as 2 or 3 percent at times. They could check a random sample of the loan pool or focus on those loans most likely to be problematic. The loan examiners—who may work in-house at the securitizing institution or a third-party company—would use three main criteria when judging the quality of each loan: to what extent did the loan comply with the originator's and sometimes the securitizer's stated criteria for who qualifies for a loan; did it comply with federal and state laws; and to what extent were there 'compensating factors' that may offset any non-compliant parts of the loan. For example, an applicant with a lower income than required may have considerable savings in the bank. The examiner would compile a report for the pool as a whole based the results of this sample. With that knowledge, the securitizer could eliminate loans that did not meet the guidelines and possibly renegotiate the price paid to the originator.[5]

Clayton Holdings is a third-party company that examines loan pools for banks. Their information has been instrumental in some civil cases and investigations surrounding the 2008 financial crisis. Clayton's executives told the Congressional Financial Crisis Inquiry Commission that in the eighteen months preceding June 30, 2007, it examined 911,039 loans for Citigroup Inc., Credit Suisse Group AG, Deutsche Bank AG, Goldman Sachs Group Inc., J.P. Morgan, Lehman Brothers, Merrill Lynch, UBS (Union Bank of Switzerland) Group AG and Washington Mutual. Out of these nearly one million loans, 54 percent met all guidelines (known as Grade 1), 18 percent were approved with compensating factors, such as extra savings or assets (known as Grade 2), and 39 percent were deficient without sufficient mitigating factors (known as Grade 3). However, the securitizers can choose to "wave in" loans anyway, and the banks did so for 39 percent of those found deficient, or 11 percent of the total pool.[6] One possible reason for waiving in so many of these loans was that securitizers were desperate for them, according to Clayton President Keith Johnson.[7]

The securitizer banks created sales statements, known as prospectuses, in which they described underlying loan to pool to potential investors. According to Clayton's data, they knowingly provided false information in these statements. "Prospectuses indicated that the loans in the pools either met guidelines outright or had compensating factors, even though Clayton's records show that only a portion of the loans were sampled, and that of those that were sampled, a substantial percentage of Grade 3 loans were waved in," according to the Financial Crisis Inquiry Commission (FCIC) report.[8] Column E of figure 6.1 shows high waiver rates at many of the major investment banks shortly before the crash. Recalling our earlier definition of fraud as knowingly providing false or misleading information that causes a purchaser to lose money, this testimony by Clayton should have pricked up the ears of government prosecutors if they were looking for evidence in a criminal investigation. Indeed, Clayton's data has been used in various non-criminal cases. Clayton lays out very clearly the knowingly and misleading components of the securitizer banks' activity, and clearly many people lost money investing in mortgage-backed securities in the financial crisis of 2008. Maybe they did

Rejected Loans Waived in by Selected Banks

From January 2006 through June 2007, Clayton rejected 28% of the mortgages it reviewed. Of these, 39% were waived in anyway.

Financial Institution	A ACCEPTED LOANS *(Event 1 & 2)/ Total pool of loans*	B REJECTED LOANS *(Event 3)/ Total pool of loans*	C REJECTED LOANS WAIVED IN BY FINANCIAL INSTITUTIONS	D REJECTED LOANS AFTER WAIVERS (B–C)	E FINANCIAL INSTITUTION WAIVER RATE (C/B)
Citigroup	58%	42%	13%	29%	31%
Credit Suisse	68	32	11	21	33
Deutsche	65	35	17	17	50
Goldman	77	23	7	16	29
JP Morgan	73	27	14	13	51
Lehman	74	26	10	16	37
Merrill	77	23	7	16	32
UBS	80	20	6	13	33
WaMu	73	27	8	19	29
Total Bank Sample	**72%**	**28%**	**11%**	**17%**	**39%**

Figure 6.1 Rejected Loans Waived In, by Bank.
Source: United States Financial Crisis Inquiry Commission, "The Financial Crisis Inquiry Report: Final Report of the National Commission on the Causes of the Financial and Economic Crisis in the United States—Resource Library," https://fcic.law.stanford.edu/resource/graphics, accessed July 27, 2021.

look into Clayton's testimony, and maybe it would have been helpful in making a criminal case, but due to the lack of a thorough criminal investigation made known to the public, we will never know.

COUNTRYWIDE CHAIRMAN, CEO AND CO-FOUNDER ANGELO MOZILO AND BANK OF AMERICA CHAIRMAN AND CEO KENNETH LEWIS

In January 2008, Bank of America Corporation (BofA) bought Countrywide Financial Corporation as it was collapsing under the weight of the subprime mortgage crisis that it had been instrumental in fueling. Countrywide reported a $1.2 billion loss in the third quarter of 2007 after twenty-five years of profit, and saw its shares drop 79 percent in 2007. At the time of the BofA purchase, a *CNN Money* article reported "Bank of America Chairman and

CEO Kenneth Lewis suggested he was aware of the troubles that his firm was taking on, but said acquiring Countrywide was a 'rare opportunity' for his company." Lewis said his company was obtaining a valuable mortgage platform for a deeply discounted price.[9]

The office of Assistant U.S. Attorney Stephen A. Cazares, of the Central District of California, began a grand jury investigation of the former Countrywide executive Angelo Mozilo in 2008. The district covers Riverside, San Bernardino, Orange, Los Angeles, San Luis Obispo, Santa Barbara, Ventura, and Calabasas, California—the former home of Countrywide. However, by 2011, California prosecutors wound down the case without filing any criminal charges. "Sometimes the public thinks all you have to do is to indict someone and that's it," an anonymous federal source told the *Washington Post*, regarding the Mozilo case. "But you have to be able to prove your case, and it can be worse losing a case than not bringing one at all."[10] This quote is yet another note in the song of caution sung by the Justice Department. The question is, whom is it worse for:; the Justice Department, the American people, or the economy?

The Justice Department may have different goals depending on the political philosophy of those elected and appointed to run it. Which laws it enforces and how aggressively it does so is always a decision to be made, hence the importance of studying the details of how prosecutors exercise this discretionary power. Certainly, it could be worse for the Department's reputation and operation if it continues to lose cases or does so in a way that harms many Americans, such as Enron's accounting firm Arthur Andersen going out of business, which punished many innocent employees and others. However, in cases where there is strong evidence and the very trust in the rule of law and the judicial system hangs in the balance, the public needs more than vague statements from prosecutors. The Securities and Exchange Commission settled with Mozilo in late 2010 for $67.5 million, $45 million of which he repaid to shareholders based on what the government said were "ill-gotten gains."[11] This settlement avoided a civil trial on charges of fraud and insider trading, and the Justice Department simply dropped any criminal inquiry.

The office of Preet Bharara, the U.S. Attorney for the Southern District of New York, brought civil charges against Bank of America as Countrywide's new owner, as well as against former Countrywide executive Rebecca Mairone—who was not a top executive like Mozilo—in October 2012 for Countrywide's fraudulent activity. A Manhattan court found Mairone and Bank of America guilty in this civil case, which centered on a Countrywide program, headed by Mairone, known as "The Hustle."[12] The Hustle is the HSSL or High-Speed Swim Lane mortgage lending program of 2007 that quickly processed loans removing traditional "toll gates" slowing down the lending process. These gates were important in preventing fraud, according to the complaint.[13] Bharara released a statement after the verdict was handed down in October 2013 saying that Countrywide

> treated quality control and underwriting as a joke . . . In a rush to feed at the trough of easy mortgage money on the eve of the financial crisis, Bank of America purchased Countrywide, thinking it had gobbled up a cash cow. That profit, however, was built on fraud, as the jury unanimously found.[14]

Bharara's statement also said, "This Office will never hesitate to go to trial to expose fraudulent corporate conduct and to hold companies accountable, particularly when it has caused such harm to the public."[15] However, his tough talk ultimately rings hollow. His office sought no criminal charges against any Countrywide or BofA official, which is arguably the only disincentive for future corporate criminals from megabanks who can afford to pay fines as the cost of doing business. Perhaps vindicating Bharara's decision not to pursue criminal charges, in 2016, an appeals court overturned the decision because it said the government failed to prove intent to defraud. It instead treated the case as a lesser breach of contract matter.[16]

The SEC's civil case was more appropriately targeted. It alleged that Mozilo and two other top Countrywide executives—David Sambol, chief operating officer and president, and Eric Sieracki, chief financial officer—failed to disclose in 2005, 2006, and 2007 the increasingly lowering lending standards, when describing the company's policies in mandatory disclosure forms to the government. In its history, Countrywide made loans that conformed to more conservative standards set by the then-government sponsored entities, Fannie Mae and Freddie Mac. However, Countrywide approached the early twenty-first century booming mortgage market with a "supermarket strategy," the complaint said, seeking to match any lending standard offered by other lenders. For example, if a competitor would write a loan for no money down to someone with a low credit score, Countrywide would offer that deal as well. As another example, the complaint alleged that Mozilo and Sambol knew as of June 2006 that an internal audit showed that 50 percent of the "stated income loans"—meaning the borrower need not show proof of income at the time of receiving the loan—showed that borrowers' incomes were inflated by 10 percent or more. In other words, half of these loans, sometimes called "liars' loans," were, not surprisingly, based on lies. Of those "liars' loans," 69 percent had more than 50 percent difference in stated and actual income, as per Internal Revenue Service filings. Some people blame the "liars," the individuals taking out these mortgages. Whether or not they deserve some of the blame, certainly the balance of responsibility must go to the lending institution. Firstly, as stated, Countrywide had a policy of matching any other bank's best offer. Additionally, their HSSL policy shows how willing they were to make a loan in almost any circumstance. Also, the most sophisticated home mortgage borrower is still at an information disadvantage compared to the bankers. For example, the borrower may not know that a loan officer's manager is pushing him to make a certain number of loans per month, or a certain number of subprime loans per month. It is safe to say that most borrowers are not nearly as sophisticated and educated about home mortgage products as those people whose job it is to create mortgage loans. It defies logic to argue that most Americans understand the various details and myriad complexities involved in mortgage policies. People go to a mortgage broker to get a mortgage, not only because they are the ones empowered to lend, but also because they are the experts. Why not trust the expert when he says you should report a higher than accurate income or take out a mortgage with a low introductory rate that balloons in two years? He may have reassured you that even if you can't afford the higher rate after the introductory period, you could always sell or refinance because it's unlikely the value of your home would go down in such a booming market. The likelihood of an informational imbalance must put the burden on the lender, not the borrower, for selling these products while knowing the danger they could cause, and did, in fact cause when the subprime mortgage bubble burst. Most importantly, we can see from programs like the HSSL that internal policies required this kind of indiscriminate and aggressive sale of mortgages by its employees because the lending institution made tremendous profits from origination fees while avoiding any risk of non-repayment by selling off the loans to securitizers.

The fraudulent acts occurred when the results of Countrywide's internal investigation were not disclosed to investors, according to the SEC complaint. By 2006, the government alleges, Mozilo and Sambol were aware that many of the loans they were making would not be sellable to securitizers, but this key information was not disclosed to investors. By making so many risky home loans that were not sellable to securitizers, Countrywide was taking significant risk with its financial health. This information was absolutely owed to investors in the company, but Mozilo and the other executives signed forms in which this important or "material" information about the company's practices and risks were not disclosed, according to the complaint.[17] Additionally, the government charged:

> Indeed, Mozilo, Sieracki and Sambol each made public statements from 2005 through 2007 that were intended to mislead investors about the increasingly aggressive underwriting at Countrywide and the financial consequences of those widened underwriting guidelines.[18]

This type of information withholding seems like a blatant example of what fraud statutes were designed to prevent, and it is the federal government itself announcing the proof. It stretches the imagination why this wouldn't make a compelling case for criminal fraud. Certainly, the public was owed a better explanation in this case.

LEHMAN BROTHERS CEO RICHARD "DICK" FULD

For twenty years, Lehman Brothers had been heavily involved in the mortgage origination, underwriting, and securitization business. In March 2006, Lehman CEO Dick Fuld announced to the company that it would hold more mortgage assets on its books as long-term investments. The investment bank increased its mortgage-related investments to $111 billion in 2007 from $67 billion in 2006, and Lehman continued to up its ante on real estate into early 2008 (before it declared bankruptcy in September 2008). However, this investment strategy ignored the firm's own risk policies and advice from risk managers. For example, the firm's Securities and Exchange Commission auditor said Lehman should begin selling some of its real estate investments to avoid losses. Instead, the firm ignored this warning and employed an "accounting gimmick," as described by Lehman executives. Shortly before each reporting period, Lehman would employ a technique known as "Repo 105" that moved $50 billion in assets off its balance sheets temporarily, making the company appear more financially stable to its shareholders. Lehman's own president and chief operating officer as of June 2008, Bart McDade, wrote in an email that the Repo 105 transactions were "another drug we R on." Lehman's auditor, Ernst & Young Global Ltd., was aware of the Repo 105 scheme but did not question the bank's failure to disclose it. The accounting firm maintained it was not required to do so.[19,20] Fuld told the United States House of Representatives' Financial Services Committee on April 20, 2010 that

> I have absolutely no recollection whatsoever of hearing anything about Repo 105 transactions while I was CEO of Lehman. Nor do I have any recollection of seeing documents that related to Repo 105 transactions. The first time I recall ever hearing the term "Repo 105" was a year after the bankruptcy filing in connection with questions raised by the Examiner.[21]

Anton R. Valukas, Lehman's bankruptcy examiner also testified before the House committee on April 20, 2010. He told the committee that Lehman's usage of the Repo 105 transaction in the way it did without disclosure was not appropriate. "In light of the market's focus on the leverage of investment banks in late 2007 and 2008, I found that sufficient evidence exists for a judge or jury to find that Lehman's reported net leverage ratio was materially misleading during that period."[22] When asked if Fuld's statement that he did not know about the Repo 105 transaction was credible, Valukas replied:

> We concluded in the report that a fact finder could conclude that in fact he did know and acted upon information he knew or should have known. There was at least one witness who testified that he discussed Repo 105 transactions with him. In the magnitude of those transactions, there were documents that were sent to him by e-mail and otherwise which reflected the Repo 105 transactions which were dealing with balance sheet which were a great issue and concern to Lehman Brothers at the time. The two presidents of Lehman Brothers acknowledged they knew about Repo 105. The three CFOs during that period of time claim they knew about Repo 105 and numerous other executives. Mr. Fuld's position was that he did not know about it. If an action is brought, someone will determine whether that is or is not credible.[23]

This example seems to be a slam dunk for the government. Valukas did their job for them. Valukas is a litigator and senior partner at the prominent law firm Jenner & Block, and a former United States Attorney who was appointed by the court to lead the Lehman bankruptcy examination, which was the largest such case in United States History.[24] The extensive "Valukas Report," seems to provide a gold mine for federal prosecutors. An explanation is also sorely needed in this case.

CITIGROUP

In November 2007, Richard M. Bowen III, a senior vice president at CitiFinancial Mortgage, a division of Citigroup, emailed warnings to company executives, including Executive Committee Chairman and former Clinton Treasury Secretary Robert Rubin. As head of correspondent lending in the Consumer Lending Group, Bowen had been speaking out since June 2006 about problems with the bank's guarantees made to Fannie Mae, Freddie Mac, and others purchasing loan packages for sale to investors. Bowen's group at Citi included 220 underwriters who would examine a small sample of these mortgage loans worth approximately $50 billion each year purchased from 1,600 originators. Citi had not done the original underwriting on these loans, but through examining a sample of them, it would ensure to investors that the loans adhered to Citi's credit standards. Bowen told the FCIC that an increased volume of loans and staffing limitations made this task more difficult. Before selling the bundle of loans as investment products, Citi policy demanded that 95 percent or more of the loans sold adhere to bank credit standards and contain enough documentation to prove it. Otherwise, Citi could demand that the originator repurchase the loans, like a money-back guarantee. Bowen told the Congressional Financial Crisis Inquiry Commission that he began warning managers in mid-2006 that he found 60 percent of the loans sold were defective, when Citi said they were not. He worried that this could trigger massive losses for the bank, as these loans would be subject to repurchase agreements. Bowen continued his warnings through 2006 to no avail. Yet the rate of defective mortgages climbed to 80 percent, he told the Commission. During this time, he also watched as Citi's Wall Street Chief Risk Officer overturned the decision on many loan files from "denied" to "approved" for sale. "In the sample on one $300+ million Merrill Lynch subprime pool the underwriters turned down 716 mortgages as not meeting Citi policy guidelines," Bowen told the FCIC. "The Wall Street Chief Risk Officer personally changed 260 of these 'turn downs' to 'approved.' The pool was purchased."[25]

Bowen then emailed the highest level of bank management, asking for an internal investigation outside of the Consumer Lending Group, as his warnings within the group had fallen on mostly deaf ears. Bowen's direct manager was also concerned and continued to press for changes. By early 2007, however, the manager's responsibilities were distributed to others and Bowen then retired.[26] It is hard to see how Citi executives were not willfully ignoring that the bank was lying to investors in saying its investment products met its standards. Why wouldn't federal prosecutors take some action here? Some explanation is owed.

AIG FINANCIAL PRODUCTS CEO JOSEPH J. CASSANO

American International Group (AIG), the largest insurance company in the world as of 2004, had a problem child. AIG had a AAA credit rating. This highest possible rating was exceptionally rare for a private company, and it allowed AIG to borrow money for low interest rates. Capitalizing on its parent's solid financial footing, a unit of the company, AIG Financial Products (FP), began a lucrative business issuing Credit Default Swaps for Wall Street in 1998. Investors in CDOs[27] or other similar financial products could buy these Credit Default Swap (CDS) contracts to hedge against any potential losses in the value of the CDO. In other words, in exchange for paying a regular premium to AIG, investors could guarantee they would receive a payout if the value of their investment dropped or another related "event" occurred. This isn't too far from the way many insurance policies work, except instead of promising a payment to help you fix your car if it is damaged so long as you pay your monthly premium, CDS are more like hedging bets in Las Vegas. Essentially, AIG was betting mortgage-related investment projects would never drop much in value because the housing market would never go down enough for them to do so. Those buying the CDS were hedging their bets in case the market went up or down. AIG made hundreds of millions of dollars each year on these CDS contracts.[28] (This process is also very condescendingly spelled out to the only female in the room in the movie *Too Big to Fail*, for those who want an audio-visual explanation with celebrities.)

However, since CDS policies were not actually a regulated type of insurance, they were not subject to requirements that the insurer have a reserve pool of money for payouts. Also, by having CDS contracts on these mortgage investments, banks were subject to much lower requirements to hold cash on their own books. Lower requirements for cash meant more money that could be invested for higher returns. Goldman Sachs was AIG's biggest customer for these policies.[29] Banks and hedge funds sold CDS policies as well, but they were on both sides of these bets, whereas AIG only sold them. This was a fine business model for AIG, so long as the assets—home mortgages—underlying the bonds they insured maintained steady payments. However, when the subprime mortgage crisis hit and mortgage-related bonds lost value en masse, AIG could not pay out on so many policies at once. In hindsight, this seems like a disaster waiting to happen, but many will say no one could have foreseen the traditionally reliable housing marking crashing so dramatically. Clearly there was no way to know they would be in trouble, right?

In 2005, before the worst of the crisis hit, AIG lost its AAA credit rating when auditors discovered it inflated its earnings in the previous five years by $3.9 billion. Maurice "Hank" Greenberg, who had been CEO for thirty-eight years and was forced out by the company's board, told the Financial Crisis Inquiry Commission that the Financial Products group should have stopped writing these risky CDS policies at that time. Cassano, head of the Financial Products group, allowed his team to write another $36 billion in CDS contracts for another year, despite warnings from some of his executives about the increasingly precarious state of the housing market. Meanwhile Cassano personally took home at least thirty-eight million dollars in each year between 2002 and 2007.[30] Cassano knew about risks the company was taking that were not disclosed to his executives or investors via SEC filings, as they are legally required to do.[31] AIG Financial Products executive Gene Park said that by June 2007, most executives at AIG knew the company would need to pay out if many borrowers defaulted on their loans. However, they did not know that payouts would be triggered if the market value of the bonds declined or credit rating agencies downgraded the bonds. This meant that payouts may be owed even if no cash losses occurred. Cassano was aware of this provision, but AIG's regulator, the Office of Thrift Supervision was not.[32] The FCIC also reported that Cassano was generally less than cooperative with the regulator.[33]

Investment bank Goldman Sachs officially requested a $1.8 billion payout, claiming the market value of $20 billion in insured CDO had dropped 15 percent. AIG disagreed with this calculation, a battle that was likely predictable since there was little transparency or liquidity in this type of deal. It wasn't exactly the New York Stock Exchange with a ticker in Times Square. On the same day as this collateral request, Goldman purchased a $100 million contract from another company insuring against the possibility that AIG might default on its obligations; a hedge on a hedge. In the next year, Goldman would continue to purchase CDS contracts against AIG, while battling the company for payouts daily. By this point, AIG FP had insured $79 billion in bonds that were mostly backed by subprime and Alt-A (nearly subprime) home loans. AIG's parent company only reported $95.8 billion in capital and AIG FP had done almost no hedging of its own because AIG FP executives believed "there could never be losses." AIG initially purchased a $150 million hedge, but had begun to lose money on it, so Cassano refused to spend any more. "I don't think the world is going to blow up," Park quoted Cassano as saying.[34] The world didn't so much blow up as implode. In 2007, the CDS contracts threatened to take down the entire company that had only a few years prior been rated AAA. On a quarterly earnings call with investors and analysts in November 2007, AIG disclosed a $352 million claim for payout on its CDS portfolio. The company was using a new model—in the sense that it never had one before, not that it replaced an old one—to mark the current value of its CDS portfolio. AIG had previously relied on companies like Goldman—one that would demand a payout—to let them know when a market price changed. That is like if my car insurance company relied on my word to decide how much I should get paid if my car was totaled.

On the earnings call, Cassano said AIG had more than enough money to make any payouts that may be necessary, but he believed it was highly unlikely they would have to pay. However, Cassano did not disclose on the call that AIG's private auditor, PricewaterhouseCoopers LLP, pointed out various significant problems with the new model and questioned its relevance. By the end of the month, the model was abandoned.[35] On a December 5 call, an analyst asked about disputes with banks regarding payouts and the valuation model mentioned in the November call. Cassano responded that there was no hostile disagreement about payouts owed. Sometimes companies came calling with higher requests than AIG believed they owed, and either the requesting company would "go away" or they would negotiate a compromise. According to the Financial Crisis Inquiry Commission:

> Cassano did not reveal the $2 billion collateral posted to Goldman, the several hundred million dollars posted to other counterparties, and the daily demands from Goldman and the others for additional cash . . . Investors . . . did not know that AIG's earnings were overstated by $3.6 billion—and they would not learn that information until February 11, 2008.[36]

Outside auditors from a private accounting firm concluded in late 2007 that AIG's publicly reported numbers were wrong. They cited a lack of effective and experienced leadership at AIG FP. They agreed to continue auditing AIG as long as Cassano did not "interfere in the process." When the overstated earnings were announced on February 11, 2008, the ratings agencies again downgraded AIG. Goldman continued to demand more payments from AIG and buy hedges against its failure at the same time. On February 28, AIG announced a net loss of $5.29 billion, mostly due to AIG FP's $11.12 billion in losses in value, as well as $2.6 billion in losses by another AIG subsidiary that had been investing in mortgage-backed securities directly. Cassano's retirement was also announced that day. However, he was still retained as a consultant making a million dollars a month in addition to the $300 million he had earned between 1987 and 2008.[37]

By September 2008, AIG FP was severely weighing down AIG. Although the company had a trillion dollars in assets, most of the liquid assets were held by more regulated subsidiaries that could not provide cash for AIG FP. The subsidiary now faced $23.4 billion in requests for payment. At the same time, the banks that lend money to other companies to operate daily—the lifeblood of the financial industry—refused to provide AIG with cash, and the AIG subsidiary that had invested $75 billion in mortgage-backed securities hemorrhaged billions as well as MBS values continued to tank. Lastly, Goldman Sachs analysts had written a report in August warning clients not to invest in AIG due to severe losses and another potential ratings downgrade for AIG, as if Goldman was an unbiased observer. The insurer was rapidly running out of funding, having only days to live, particularly if it was downgraded again. Fearing a run on AIG's remaining assets and a subsequent bankruptcy, which would in turn cause massive losses for the twelve largest banks in the United States and Europe, AIG received an $85 billion loan from the Federal Reserve, which could only lend to non-banks like AIG in this way under extreme circumstances. The government later added another $49.1 billion to prop up AIG under the congressionally approved TARP bailout program.[38] While Goldman seems like the bully in this scenario, AIG FP was not a helpless middle schooler on the playground. Cassano knew what he was doing, did not disclose it properly, and caused economic havoc in the process. What logical reason did federal prosecutors have for thinking they couldn't make a good case here?

RATINGS AGENCIES

When banks packaged and sold mortgage-backed securities and CDOs, they needed ratings for the various components of these investment products.

After all, investors want to know how much risk they can expect. Some investment managers, such as those in charge of a public employee retirement fund or a university endowment, will be required to invest only in AAA-rated products—ostensibly the safest one could get—since they are playing with the ability for teachers to retire or schools to build new libraries. Many investors, even those willing to risk losing money in turn for higher returns, will only invest in the BBB-rated or higher slices of MBS or CDO. A rating of BBB or higher is considered "investment grade."[39] The ratings range all the way down to DDD. Regardless, investors want to know what they can expect.

Representative Henry A. Waxman, Chairman of the House Committee on Oversight and Government Reform, said at an October 22, 2008 hearing on the rating agencies' role in the financial crisis that although the CEOs of the three major ratings agencies—Standard & Poor's, Moody's and Fitch—would testify that they could not have foreseen the crisis, documentary evidence obtained by his committee would prove otherwise.[40] The problem for the three major agencies was they portrayed themselves as independent assessors. They were anything but independent. Indeed, they were paid by the banks for rating their investment products. This is a clear conflict of interest, and it is almost impossible to imagine how they could operate with two fundamentally opposed directives—make money and provide "objective" bond ratings.

Standard & Poor's, for example, charged hundreds of thousands of dollars for each individual MBS or CDO it rated and continued to monitor. The global CDO rating division saw revenues of ninety-six million dollars in 2005 grow to $182 million in 2006 and to $203 million in 2007. Another division rating similar bonds took in revenues of more than $278 million in 2006 and $243 million in 2007. If a bank does not like the policies of one rating agency, it can threaten to take its business elsewhere. Therefore, banks have the agencies at a financial gunpoint. Clearly, the loss of any deal, let alone all of a bank's business, would be a major loss to the agency.

In February 2013, the Justice Department filed a civil case against Standard & Poor's and its parent company, McGraw-Hill Companies, Inc., for mail fraud, wire fraud, and financial institution fraud under the Financial Institutions Reform, Recovery, and Enforcement Act of 1989. "To date, the government has identified more than $5 billion in losses suffered by federally insured financial institutions in connection with the failure of CDOs rated by S&P from March to October 2007," according to a Justice Department press release.[41] The government alleged that S&P represented its ratings as "objective, independent and uninfluenced by any conflict of interest," and therefore knowingly and intentionally defrauded investors who relied on them. Although the company claimed that any misstatements were "mere puffery," internal emails cited in the complaint show debates about lowering rating standards to remain competitive with Moody's. Meanwhile the company's executives continued to tout its objectivity in rating and monitoring mortgage-related securities.[42] Employees doing the ratings work were keenly aware of the dangers of the perverse incentive system and corporate policies. The following except from the complaint deserves to be included in its entirety:

> On or about April 5, 2007, two S&P CDO analysts engage in an instant message exchange expressing their belief that the S&P CDO rating model severely underestimated credit risks:
>
> [Analyst] btw that deal is ridiculous
>
> [Analyst] I know right . . . model def[initely] does not capture half of the . . . risk
>
> [Analyst] We should not be rating it
>
> [Analyst] we rate every deal . . . it could be structured by cows and we would rate it
>
> [Analyst] but there's a lot of risk associated with it—I personally don't feel comfy signing off as a committee member.[43]

The complaint lays out the myriad ways in which Standard & Poor's "scheme to defraud investors" breaks the Financial Institutions Reform, Recovery and Enforcement Act (FIRREA) law. It also notes that FIRREA, a savings and loan crisis-era statute enacted to combat this very type of behavior, can carry criminal, as well as civil penalties.[44] But by February 2015, Standard & Poor's settled this and other cases with nineteen states and the District of Columbia for a total of $1.5 billion. Why not pursue charges against the individuals responsible for this company that knowingly mislead investors, causing massive losses? In portraying themselves as independent arbiters of bond quality and an entire financial industry relying on these ratings, one could argue the agencies should be an obvious target for serious and meaningful law enforcement efforts. Yet the entire effort to hold them accountable went out with a whimper. A $1.5 billion settlement makes a good headline, prosecutors look tough without trying too hard, and everyone goes home. This is simply not good enough as an explanation.

Various industry executives knew important and relevant facts about their company's financial products and chose not to disclose them, causing millions in losses. These seem to be textbook examples of criminal fraud, at least in theory. So why didn't any of these people face criminal prosecution? To be sure, prosecuting financial crime is difficult. It may be true that the

2008 crisis was in some ways more complicated than previous ones. The more complicated the scheme, ostensibly, the harder it would be to prosecute. There's no reason to believe government prosecutors aren't smart or skilled enough. Indeed, they are consistently picked from the most prestigious law schools. In a criminal trial, a jury would not necessarily be familiar with the financial products involved. But there are ways to tell the stories of the 2008 crisis in a manner so the average juror could not only understand but feel enraged and wronged by these people. Narrative and emotion, after all, is what sways the jury. Simply put, the story would be told about people who lied and said their product was good when they knew it was actually dangerous. The finance industry likes to compare itself to car salesmen and promotes a *caveat emptor* mentality. Unfortunately for them, there is only so far that idea will take them until they run afoul of criminal fraud statutes. The evidence I have offered in this chapter makes a total lack of criminal prosecution after the 2008 financial crisis hard to defend. Department prosecutors often say they simply follow the evidence, but the idea of prosecutorial discretion proves that can't possibly be the end of the story. The problem for victims of financial fraud is not so much the ability to make a criminal case against a powerful entity or individual, as the willingness to do so. In subsequent chapters, I will show why government prosecutors lost this willingness after 2008, but not in previous crises.

NOTES

1. Anonymous interview.
2. Moon interview.
3. Henning, Perter J. December 13, 2010. "The Difficulty of Proving Financial Crimes."
4. House Financial Services Committee hearing, April 20, 2010.
5. FCIC Report, p. 166.
6. FCIC Report, pp. 166–167.
7. FCIC Report, p. 166.
8. FCIC Report, p. 167.
9. Ellis, "Countrywide Rescue: $4 Billion."
10. Reckard, "Criminal Probe Dropped against Countrywide CEO Angelo Mozilo."
11. Reckard, "Criminal Probe Dropped against Countrywide CEO Angelo Mozilo."
12. Breslow, "Bank of America Liable for Mortgage 'Hustle' Program."
13. U.S. v. Bank of American Corporation, successor to Countrywide Financial Corporation, 12 Civ 1422.
14. Department of Justice, Southern District of New York, "Statement of Manhattan U.S. Attorney Preet Bharara on the Countrywide, Bank of America, and Rebecca Mairone Verdict,." October 23, 2013.

15. Department of Justice, Southern District of New York, "Statement of Manhattan U.S. Attorney Preet Bharara on the Countrywide, Bank of America, and Rebecca Mairone Verdict,." October 23, 2013.
16. Lane, "Appeals Court Overturns Bank of America's $1.27 Billion Fine in 'Hustle' Case."
17. SEC v. Mozilo, Sambol, Sieracki, CV09–03994, complaint.
18. SEC v. Mozilo, Sambol, Sieracki, CV09–03994, complaint.
19. FCIC Report, p. 177.
20. Testimony of Anton R. Valukas, Examiner, Lehman Brothers Bankruptcy, Committee on Banking, Housing, & Urban Affairs Subcommittee on Securities, Insurance, and Investment United States Senate, April 6, 2011.
21. Fuld Testimony, House Financial Services Committee, April 20, 2010.
22. Testimony of Anton R. Valukas, Examiner, Lehman Brothers Bankruptcy, House Financial Services Committee, April 20, 2010.
23. Testimony of Anton R. Valukas, Examiner, Lehman Brothers Bankruptcy, House Financial Services Committee, April 20, 2010.
24. Valukas, "Jenner & Block—People."
25. Bowen FCIC testimony.
26. Bowen FCIC testimony.
27. See chapter 5 for explanation of CDO, or Collateralized Debt Obligations.
28. Sorkin, *Too Big to Fail*.
29. FCIC Report, pp. 139–141.
30. FCIC Report, pp. 141, 200, 201.
31. FCIC Report, p. 202.
32. FCIC Report, pp. 201–202, 243.
33. FCIC Report, p. 351.
34. FCIC Report, p. 267.
35. FCIC Report, pp. 269, 270, 271.
36. FCIC Report, p. 272.
37. FCIC Report, pp. 273, 274.
38. FCIC Report, p. 350.
39. United States of America v. McGraw Hill Companies and Standard & Poor's Financial Services LCC, CV13–00779, complaint.
40. Opening Statement of Rep. Henry A. Waxman Chairman, Committee on Oversight and Government Reform Credit Rating Agencies and the Financial Crisis October 22, 2008.
41. Department of Justice, Office of Public Affairs, "Department of Justice Sues Standard & Poor's for Fraud in Rating Mortgage-Backed Securities in the Years Leading Up to the Financial Crisis," February 5, 2013.
42. United States of America v. McGraw Hill Companies and Standard & Poor's Financial Services LCC, CV13–00779, complaint.
43. United States of America v. McGraw Hill Companies and Standard & Poor's Financial Services LCC, CV13–00779, complaint.
44. United States of America v. McGraw Hill Companies and Standard & Poor's Financial Services LCC, CV13–00779, complaint.

Chapter 7

Prosecutors' Incentives

Prosecutors espouse the idea that the Justice System is based on a dispassionate application of the law and facts. However, we have already established that it is impossible for every crime to be prosecuted, so there must be some choice involved. Prosecutors, in deciding whom to bring charges against, respond to incentives like everyone else. There are both personal and institutional incentives for Justice Department prosecutors, and they work in unison to shape prosecutorial behavior. It is important to clarify that the incentive structure faced here is for non-politically appointed prosecutors. Those that work at U.S. Attorney's Offices are known as Assistant U.S. Attorneys. Others work at Department of Justice Headquarters in Washington, DC, known as "Main Justice." The politically appointed people are only those in top leadership positions at the 94 Districts and Main Justice. Their leadership will certainly influence prosecutors working below them, but their incentives are different. Also, the reader should keep in mind that although I discuss incentives for individual prosecutors, they are not making cases alone. A team of prosecutors would be working on a case together, as a federal judge and former U.S. Attorney's Office supervisor and prosecutor will note later in this chapter.

While a case may reach a courtroom, which would be controlled by judicial oversight, the decision about whom to charge with what crimes are not subject to judicial review. Judges will largely defer to prosecutorial discretion, except in clear cases in which motives based on race, religion or bad faith can be attributed to the prosecutor.[1] Prosecutorial decision making is also not made public unless charges are filed. Considering that the vast majority of cases never reach a courtroom, as they are settled, and the decision-making process before charges are filed is not entirely made public even in cases that are filed, prosecutors operate outside of the public spotlight and without much oversight. Additionally, prosecutors have options beyond simply the decision to prosecute. For example, deferred prosecution—an agreement between the government and the accused party to reform behavior in lieu of prosecution—was originally created as an alternative to prison for juvenile and drug offenders. Contrasting Buell's argument in an earlier chapter, legal scholar Benjamin M. Greenblum argues this practice gives prosecutors too much power, with the result being unfair punishment for companies and innocent parties within companies, all outside judicial review.[2] Legal scholar Geraldine Szott Moohr argues that since approximately 95 percent of people charged with federal crimes settle out of court, the United States is not quite the adversarial legal system that we imagine. Instead, it bears some similarities to the French inquisitorial system, in which "the ultimate issue of guilt or innocence is determined through an official inquiry that is initiated and conducted by the state. In this system, the trial is most accurately characterized as a continuation of the official investigation. The investigation, rather than the trial, is paramount."[3] However, the French system also calls for more supervision in prosecutorial decision making, while American prosecutors are largely unrestrained. U.S. prosecutors' power to arrange guilty pleas outside the public light of a trial can result in inconsistent sentences, creating disrespect for and mistrust of the law, as well as the inability to publicly display and clarify often opaque white-collar crime, missing an opportunity to truly deter criminal behavior.[4]

Legal scholar Rachel E. Barkow emphasizes the importance of institutional structures within the Justice Department in "mediating prosecutorial impulses" and argues that some are more successful than others.[5] Institutional design influences the culture of an agency, which emphasizes some actions over others. The Justice Department's structures favor successful prosecutions.[6] "Prosecutors want to make it as easy as possible for them to win at trial, and that will-to-win can create cognitive biases in even the most well-intentioned prosecutors."[7] Don Stemen and Bruce Frederick place prosecutorial discretion within the context of criminal procedural constraints, high caseloads, limited staffing, and shared values and norms within the group of other prosecutors, judges, and defense attorneys with whom prosecutors form working relationships.[8] Additionally, professional norms and post-government service expectations can influence the way tasks are performed in an agency. A very high profile and high-risk case against a defense firm's major client or one of its executives—such as a "Too Big to Fail" bank—may be too much of a risk to take for a government prosecutor. Marc Allen Eisner and Kenneth H Meier, relying on a study of antitrust enforcement cases, argue that internal factors and not outside political control are the driving force in Justice Department decisions.[9] When the antitrust approach of the Department changed in the 1980s, they conclude that it was not the Reagan political agenda that was responsible, but instead a change in the internal structure of the Department itself, which relied increasingly on Chicago School economists' advice in decision- making processes.[10] In other words, institutional structures and incentives are important factor in prosecutorial decision making.

COST OF LIVING

Let us take a closer look at the incentives prosecutors faced after the 2008 financial crisis and how they had changed since previous crises. In terms of personal incentives, the amount of money they could make in the private sector as a partner in a prestigious law firm had drastically risen, compared to the top government salary they could expect to make. These law firms prize government experience when hiring for their white-collar defense practices, as evidenced by the staff biographies highlighting this background on firm websites. For example, elite white-collar defense firms Debevoise & Plimpton and Paul, Weiss, Rifkind, Wharton & Garrison both list approximately half of their white-collar defense attorneys as having federal government experience. They figure a former government prosecutor would be the best defensive weapon against current government prosecutions, as they would best understand the thinking and strategies of the Justice Department. However, someone who spent his or her time at the Department focused on one or two very high-profile cases that resulted in a very public loss would be a much less attractive candidate than someone who took the gettable wins, such as a multi-million- or billion-dollar settlement. Simply put, a winning record is better than a losing one. In the past, as this chapter will show, top government prosecutors would expect to earn salaries that were admittedly less than their private sector counterparts, but not drastically so. However, around the turn of the twenty-first century, that gap began to widen dramatically. Significantly more compensation is a powerful incentive. This is not to say Department attorneys aren't dedicated public servants or that some do not spend an entire career as a prosecutor, but many also move on to the private sector. An article on Harvard Law School's website says that a "significant" number people working as government prosecutors often stay in their positions for approximately five to seven years.[11]

In the case of the 2008 financial crisis, most high-level finance cases would be prosecuted by attorneys living in the country's most expensive places to live, like New York or California. New York City in a major focal point for this kind of case, as the country's major financial hub as a home to NASDAQ, American Stock Exchange, New York Mercantile Exchange, and New York Stock Exchange; as well as major investment banking and other important financial corporations. The Southern District of New York, which covers Manhattan, the Bronx, and suburban counties of New York City, has a long history with high-profile white-collar prosecutions, with the infrastructure in place to conduct them. This U.S. Attorney's office's criminal division includes Securities and Commodities Fraud Task Forces and a Complex Frauds and Cybercrime Unit.[12] Many of the white-collar defense firms have a large presence in New York as well, which makes sense their clients are there. As former United States Attorney for the Southern District of New York Geoffrey Berman told Jon Stewart in a September 2022 interview, "No financial crimes can be committed in the entire United States without some of the money running through Wall Street."[13] Adding later in the interview that the Southern District was extraordinary because "We are going toe to toe with the biggest, most formidable law firms in the country. We take them on, we are not afraid, and we have the talent." Therefore, I will focus on New York City as the strongest example of the living environment that would help shape the incentives faced by a government prosecutor.

Living in New York City is incredibly expensive. A Massachusetts Institute of Technology (MIT) study estimates that a sole provider would need to make at least $61,800 to make a bare minimum living wage for a family of four in Manhattan. The words bare minimum in that study are doing a tremendous amount of heavy lifting and is also likely an underestimate. For example, the MIT study assumes a monthly housing cost of $1,637 in 2021.[14] However, according to a report by Douglas Elliman Real Estate and Miller Samuel Real Estate Appraisers & Consultants, the average price per month to rent a New York City apartment as of May 2018 was $4,881 for a two bedroom and $7,959 for a three bedroom. Lest a reader assume this number is skewed by a handful of outrageous outliers at the high end, the median cost for a two bedroom in Manhattan as of May 2018 was $4,295 per month and $5,650 for a three-bedroom (or larger) apartment. The price doesn't drop much even when a family considers living in an outer borough in New York City. The median rental price in Brooklyn for a two-bedroom apartment was $3,092 and $3,700 for a three-bedroom (or larger) apartment as of May 2018. Northwest Queens is even more expensive, with median rates at $3,450 for a two-bedroom apartment and $3,750 for a three-bedroom (or larger) apartment as of May 2018. A family wanting to purchase a home on a government salary in New York City would be even more hard pressed, with the median 2-bedroom co-op in Manhattan selling for approximately $2 million and the median three-bedroom co-op selling for $4.025 million as of May 2018. As with the rental market, sales prices are relatively comparable in parts of Brooklyn and Queens that would allow for reasonable commutes to Manhattan.[15] These examples only consider the extremely high cost of housing in New York City. Schools, entertainment, food and other daily necessities and pleasures of life are similarly cost-inflated in New York and seem to get worse every day. A recent survey conducted by Purdue University and GoBankRates.com found that in order to "be happy" in New York City, residents feel they need to make

$220,000 per year. In San Francisco, the figure people reported needing to be happy was $319,935. Nationally, the average was much lower at $105,000.[16]

High prices in New York are not a recent phenomenon. It has long been a relatively expensive city compared to others in the United States. Comparing the federal government's Consumer Price Index for 1985 through 2015 for all United States urban areas and New York, one can see New York is consistently costlier. To be sure, there are periods of real estate slumps in New York City, but U.S. Bureau of Labor Statistics reports show that on average, New York is a relatively more expensive city compared to the national average for all urban areas.[17] Therefore, average cost of living in New York was still expensive for prosecutors pursuing white collar cases out of the Southern District of New York in the 1980s, 1990s, and early 2000s, as it was in the years following the 2008 crisis.

SALARIES

The main difference in personal incentives for attorneys prosecuting white collar cases between earlier recent crises and the 2008 crisis is the change in public versus private sector salary. The Bureau of Labor Statistics placed the average salary in 2015 (around when a prosecutor could have brought a case from the 2008 crisis) for a New York or District of Columbia metropolitan area private sector attorney at approximately $167,000.[18] The average profits per partner in one of *American Lawyer*'s top 100 firms was $1.5 million in 2015, with some earning much more.[19] In contrast, the most an Assistant United States Attorney (AUSA) could make, and only after nine or more years of service, is $136,874. However, that same experienced attorney, or even one on the job for decades, could make as little as $80,514. The average salary for an AUSA with nine or more years of experience was $108,694.[20] The most that an executive level government employee could have made in 2015 was $181,500.[21] Therefore, on average, the difference in pay for a top private firm partner and the most a government attorney could possibly make was more than $1.3 million per year in the years after the crisis.

This pay gap was not always so extreme. The pay differential between government prosecutor and law firm partner was narrower in the savings and loan crisis days. Generally, the government employee top rate in 1985 was $84,157.[22] In comparison, the Bureau of Labor Statistics reported that in 1985 the average for top-level corporate attorneys was $91,690[23] and a partner in a top firm made approximately $300,000 per year.[24] This means that in jumping from a top job in the public sector to a private sector partnership would certainly have been a boost in pay, with an average raise of about $215,000. By 1995, a partner in one of the top 100-grossing law firms averaged $446,000 per year,[25] while a senior executive attorney in the Justice Department could make up to $118,400 per year.[26] The difference in average top pay had grown to $371,000. However, in the last years of the twentieth century and the first few years of the twenty-first century, private sector lawyer income skyrocketed, while top government lawyer salaries remained flat.

In 2005, the average top-100 firm partner made $1.07 million per year, while the highest paid government attorneys could make up to $162,100.[27] By this time, the difference between government salary and private practice was enormous—almost a million dollars a year. A partner could now move into millionaire territory. It has also become harder to become an equity partner, meaning someone who shares in the firm's profits. In the past ten years, firms have turned more to non-equity partnerships. Indeed, the number of non-equity partners has almost doubled to 40 percent of the top 100 firm's partners.[28] In 1985, 36 percent of all lawyers at the top fifty law firms were equity partners. By 2017, that number had dropped to 20 percent. Prosecutors looking to become equity partners would need to become as attractive to these firms as possible. Therefore, with partnerships becoming harder to obtain and a huge jump in private income, while government salaries remained relatively flat, there is certainly a powerful incentive to choose settlement agreements over riskier prosecutions.

WHAT FIRMS WANT

To understand how important previous government experience is to these white-collar defense firms in New York or Washington, DC that were paying top dollar, I looked at what they choose to advertise on their websites in their attorney biographies. I chose law firms—Debevoise & Plimpton; Paul, Weiss, Rifkind, Wharton & Garrison; Cadwalader, Wickersham & Taft; Davis Polk; Patterson Belknap Webb & Tyler; Covington & Burling; and Ropes & Gray—with a presence in New York City and ranked National Tier 1 in white-collar criminal defense by *U.S. News and World Report*.[29] Debevoise lists forty-four attorneys on its firm website under the "white collar and regulatory defense practice" heading. Eight of those attorneys are listed as practicing outside of the United States. Out of the remaining 35, 18, or 57 percent have either Justice Department or Securities and Exchange Commission experience. Some of these attorneys have political appointee-level experience, such as former SEC Chairwoman Mary Jo White; some were career attorneys at DOJ, a U.S. Attorney's office or the SEC; and a few were both. Andrew J. Ceresney spent time as Deputy Chief Appellate Attorney for the Southern District of New York before he joined the firm in 2003. During his 10 years at Debevoise he became co-chair of the White Collar and Regulatory

Table 7.1 Change Over Time in Pay Disparity Private versus Public Sector (Amounts adjusted for inflation to 2021 dollars in parenthesis)

	Top Government Salary	*Top Private Partner Profits*	*Difference*
1985	$84,157 (a) ($212,501) (b)	$300,000 (c) ($757,516)	$215,000 ($545,015)
1995	$118,400 (d) ($205,027)	$446,000 (e) ($848,081)	$371,000 ($643,054)
2005	$162,100 (f) ($225,509)	$1,070,000 ($1,488,554)	$907,900 ($1,263,045)
2015	$181,500 (g) ($209,057)	$1,500,000 (h) ($1,727,743)	$1,318,500 ($1,518,686)

Sources: Compiled by the author using data from:
(a) General Schedule, 1985
(b) All inflation numbers translated to 2021 dollars using https://www.usinflationcalculator.com/
(c) Harper, "The Lawyer Bubble"
(d) Executive & Senior Level Pay Tables (1995), FederalPay.org
(e) Geyelin, "Law-Firm Profits Rose Slightly In 1995 as Hiring Rebounded"
(f) Executive & Senior Level Pay Tables (2005), FederalPay.org
(g) Office of Personnel, Pay & Leave Salaries & Wages, Salary Table No. 2014-ES Management
(h) Johnson, "Rich and Richer"

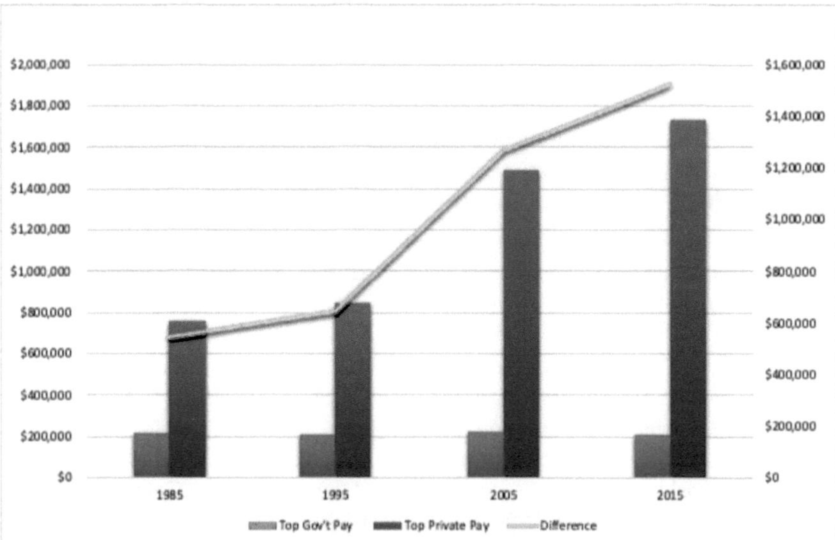

Figure 7.1 Change in Lawyer Income Over Time.
Source: Created by the author using data from Table 7.1.

Defense Group and he "played an integral role in negotiating the historic $25 billion national mortgage settlement between the federal government, 49 state attorneys general and some of the country's largest banks," according to the website.[30] Choosing to highlight this in a short online biography shows Ceresney is valued at the firm for his role in a huge monetary settlement. This shows clients that he is tough and smart, exactly the kind of lawyer they would want on their side now. Additionally, the site says from 2013 to 2017 he served as director of enforcement at the SEC and returned to the firm as a partner in 2017.[31] Again, this boasts that he led the enforcement charge against banks, so he has the best understanding of how to defend against this fight. Another white-collar litigation defense partner at Debevoise, David A. O'Neil, worked in various high-level positions at the Justice Department for eight years, including, heading the Criminal Division at the Southern District of New York.[32] David Sarratt, now a partner at the firm, worked as an Assistant United Sates Attorney for the Eastern District of New York from 2010 to 2014. James Johnson, Winston M. Paes, Mark P. Goodman, Matthew E. Fishbein, Robert N. Shwartz, Helen V. Cantwell and Matthew L. Biben all spent time as Assistant U.S. Attorneys in the Southern or Eastern Districts (covering Brooklyn, Queens, Staten Island and Long Island) of New York. Many of their website biographies boast the number of trials and appellate hearings they prosecuted while at the U.S. Attorney's offices. Like Ceresney, Goodman traveled between positions in the firm and a government prosecutor's office more than once.[33]

As for Paul, Weiss, Rifkind, Wharton & Garrison, the firm lists forty-three attorneys in its "white collar and regulatory defense practice." Nineteen of these attorneys have experience as government prosecutors, or a total of 44 percent of the practice. Like Debevoise, their biographies boast government experience, including how many cases they have tried and any major figures they have successfully prosecuted. For example, Richard C. Tarlowe spent eight years as a federal prosecutor,

> where he was Chief of the Complex Frauds and Cybercrime Unit and a member of its Securities & Commodities Fraud Task Force . . . He played a critical role in the government's crackdown on insider trading and litigated some of the most significant and high-profile securities fraud trials in the country, including the successful insider trading prosecution of Rajat Gupta, a former Goldman Sachs board member and chair of McKinsey & Co. Richard also handled cases involving public corruption, investment advisor fraud, accounting fraud and market manipulation.[34]

Various attorneys on Paul Weiss's white-collar defense roster spent approximately six years as an Assistant United States Attorney, according to the firm's website. These attorneys include Roberto Finzi, Justin Anderson, Harris Fischman, Christopher D. Frey, Michelle K. Parikh, and Adam B. Schwartz.[35] At Cadwalader, Wickersham & Taft, Jodi Avergun, chair of the firm's White-Collar Defense and Investigations Group, spent time as an Assistant U. S. Attorney in the Eastern District of New York.[36] Daniel S. Ruzumna, a partner in Patterson Bellknap's white collar defense practice, spent six years as an Assistant United States Attorney in the Southern District of New York. Joshua A. Goldberg, also a partner in the firm's white-collar litigation defense practice, served as an Assistant U.S. Attorney in the Southern District for eight years, according to the firm's website.[37] The story looks similar on the Davis Polk website. Greg Andres, a partner in the white-collar defense litigation department, served as the Deputy Assistant Attorney General at the Criminal Division at the Justice Department and Chief of the Criminal Division of the U.S. Attorney's Office for the Eastern District of New York. While at Main Justice, he served on the Financial Fraud Enforcement Task Force (and before that, the Corporate Fraud Task Force).[38] Martine M. Beamon, also a partner in Davis Polk's white collar litigation defense practice, worked as an Assistant United States Attorney for the Southern District of New York for five years. The firm's white-collar defense litigation department's partner roster also boasts Denis J. McInerny, who returned to the firm after serving as Chief of the Fraud Section (2010–2013) and then Deputy Assistant Attorney General (2013–2014) of the Criminal Division of the U.S. Department of Justice. He previously served as Deputy Chief of the Criminal Division at the U.S. Attorney's Office for the Southern District of New York (1989–1994). In between his government service, he worked at Davis Polk, representing Arthur Andersen in the infamous obstruction of justice case.[39] Michael G. McGovern, a partner in Ropes & Gray's white-collar litigation defense practice, spent seven years as an Assistant United States Attorney for the Southern District of New York.[40] Ropes & Gray Partner Joshua S. Levy also practices white collar litigation defense. He worked as a federal prosecutor for the United States Attorney's office in Massachusetts for seven years, and before that worked at Ropes & Gray, as a litigation associate.[41]

Many of the attorneys profiled here have worked at the Southern District of New York, the Eastern District of New York, or the Eastern District of Virginia, which are offices most likely to prosecute this kind of case. For example, Adam B. Schwartz is now listed as counsel at the Washington, DC office of Paul, Weiss, Rifkind, Wharton & Garrison. According to the firm's website, Schwartz spent six years as an Assistant United States Attorney at the United States Attorney's Office for the Eastern District of Virginia. He served as a federal prosecutor in the precise window of time (2008–2014) during which a case could have been prosecuted against a bank executive for the financial crisis. The firm's website says that he tried more than 40 federal cases and "argued numerous evidentiary motions and appeals." It doesn't specify the nature of these cases specifically, other than to say they involve supervision of "the investigation, indictment, and trial of complex conspiracies, homicides, public corruption and racketeering."[42] For another example, David Sarratt served as an Assistant United States Attorney in the Eastern District of New York from 2010 to 2014 and is now a partner at the elite law firm Debevoise & Plimpton. The law firm's website boasts that as an Assistant United States Attorney he successfully supervised and participated in a variety of investigations and prosecutions, successfully tried numerous cases and briefed and argued appeals to the appeals court. Although the biography on the firm's website doesn't offer specifics, it lists financial fraud among Sarratt's cases.[43]

Covington & Burling's white collar litigation defense practice boasts such partners as Lanny Breuer (Assistant Attorney General for the Criminal Division at Main Justice from 2009 – 2013) and Eric H. Holder, Jr. (United States Attorney General from February 2009 to April 2015). Both men were political appointees during the window when a case against prominent bank executives could have been brought. Although they would not have been tasked with making these difficult cases personally, they could have made a serious effort to demand and direct resources to aggressive fraud cases, but they did not as far as the public knows. President Obama established by executive order the Financial Fraud Enforcement Task Force in November 2009. The order placed the Department of Justice at the head of the task force. "But that was just a coordinating body. The only resource was one guy. It wasn't a task force. A task force is having dedicated resources," said Neil Barofsky, a task force member and Special Inspector General for the Troubled Asset Relief Program, otherwise known as "the bailout." Barofsky's insider view and the lack of meaningful prosecutions shows from the 2008 crisis shows that although some of these prominent firms boast attorneys with experiences that make them seem tough on white collar crime and perfectly poised with the right experience and location to lead their staff in a tough financial crisis criminal case, that image can be mere illusion. Others in AUSA positions often did the average five-to-seven-year stint and moved on to greener pastures.

REACTING TO JUSTICE STRATEGY

Additionally, what the defense firms are looking for in their former Justice Department attorneys have changed as the Justice Department's strategy itself has changed. This then becomes a positive feedback loop, wherein the Justice Department gravitates toward flashy settlement agreements and the private firms want attorneys who can get their clients the best outcome using this strategy. Specific to white collar crime, although many federal cases in the past were settled before they reached trial phase, prosecutors also tried some cases in a court of law. However, as discussed in a previous chapter, by the time the financial crisis hit, the Department was primed to rely on settlement agreements. After the Andersen, KPMG, Ted Stevens, and Bear Stearns embarrassments, the Department's reliance on settlements meant that white collar defense firms also had to change their strategy. Like changes in evolutionary patterns when an animal's environment changes, the defense firms had to adapt. Firms now needed former government attorneys who had experience in these types of settlement negotiations, precisely what the firms would need to defend against for their clients.

The relative ease of settlements and cautious nature of the Department as an institution during this time period creates a strong disincentive for prosecutors As Federal Judge and former Chief of the Business and Securities Fraud unit under the U.S. Attorney for the Southern District of New York, Jed Rakoff observed:

> You'd have to get into a long-term investigation still to make a high-level case. And second, you'd have already gotten the political bang with a big press conference announcing a big fine and compliance terms. You didn't have quite the same incentive to put seven Assistant U.S. Attorneys on the case.[44]

William K. Black, who as a former government regulator and attorney was instrumental in the jailing of hundreds of executives during the savings and loan crisis, also stressed the need to flip lower- and mid-level employees to testify against executives, but said that a settlement is faster and less expensive. U.S. Attorneys' offices are notoriously big on production and numbers, said Black. The chance of success in a financial fraud case is lower than others, especially considering that executives have tremendous resources to mount the best defense. "You get very low numbers if you do complicated fraud cases that are ultra fact-heavy," Black said. Prosecutors "are almost exclusively in the business of negotiating a plea deal. Many prosecutors view this case as having very little 'jury appeal' because they are more jargon paper cases." A successful prosecution, moreover, may only result in probation or little jail time. "That's the kind of thing that drives US Attorneys crazy." Similarly, Rakoff noted, "You can see why a department would be attracted to a different resource allocation."

Government attorneys want to bring high-profile cases, but losing such a case would be worse than not bringing one at all. The Bear Stearns case was difficult for the jury to understand, former Justice Department prosecutor John Moon said. "They lost their first major case they brought," he said.

"No one wants to go around losing cases. That was a big wake-up call for Justice . . . A lot of times they do go harder, their career will be better if they make a splashy case. But if you lose a splashy case you are hammered." Therefore, settlements are much safer bet.

RESOURCES

The institutional incentive structure of the Justice Department at the time works in tandem with the personal incentives for prosecutors. In addition to a change in personal monetary incentives and an increased culture of caution as notable changes between 2008 and earlier crises, significant resources moved away from white collar crime in the ensuing years. If a prosecutor must be extra cautious against a high-profile loss to please the needs of future employers, certainly having less money and no help from other agencies further increases the risk. In the previous crises, prosecutors had more resources both inside the Justice Department and from other regulators. A Justice Department Office of the Inspector General Report said in September 2005:

> In the wake of the terrorist attacks of September 11, 2001, the Justice Department, including the FBI, saw a massive shift in money and manpower to counterterrorism at the expense of other areas of law enforcement. we found that prior to 9/11, although the FBI identified counterterrorism in its top priorities, the FBI utilized the majority of its agent resources in traditional criminal investigative areas, such as white-collar crime, violent crime, organized crime, and drugs. Following 9/11, agent usage on terrorism-related matters dramatically increased.[45]

In contrast, during the savings and loan era, Congress devoted more resources to prosecutorial efforts, both legally and monetarily with the broad-based Financial Institutions Reform, Recovery and Enforcement Act (FIRREA) of 1989. The law also increased prison sentences for financial institution crimes committed after August 9, 1989; extended the statute of limitations for these crimes to ten years from five; authorized increases in FBI and prosecutorial staff; and added seventy-five million dollars annually for three years to prosecute these crimes. During the savings and loan crisis there were 1,000 FBI agents investigating crime in that industry. As of 2007, there were only 120 FBI agents covering mortgage fraud, with more than 1,800 agents, or nearly one-third of all agents in criminal programs, having moved to counterterrorism duties.[46] This was despite the fact that in September 2004, the FBI warned of an "epidemic" of mortgage fraud. According to an investigation by the *New York Times*, in the early months of the financial crisis, the FBI requested more than 1,100 agents to investigate crimes not related to national security,[47] specifically asking Congress for more money to hire new white-collar crime agents, but was continually rebuffed. It is clear Congress was as yet unwilling to shift the FBI's priorities. Likely, Congress members were simply responding to the political environment and pressures of the time to address terrorism, but a thorough analysis of Congress' role in the crisis is outside the scope of this inquiry. The *Times* writes that the bureau asked for an increase of $800 million during those years but received only $50 million more.[48] By 2008, the FBI lost 625 agents investigating white collar crime, or 36 percent of its 2001 levels.[49] Former FBI director, Robert Mueller told the Financial Crisis Inquiry Commission that the agency had asked for more resources to fight mortgage fraud during its budget process with Congress, but the Bureau did not get as much as requested, and its resources may have been insufficient.[50] However, he also said that after September 11, 2001, mortgage fraud needed to be considered "in the context of other priorities," such as terrorism. At the peak of the subprime mortgage frenzy and just before the crash, George W. Bush's Attorneys General Alberto Gonzalez (2005–2007) and Michael B. Mukasey (2007–2008) were aware of or might have done more about white-collar crime related to mortgages but terrorism was a huge focus.[51] It seems like the federal white collar crime cops had almost all left the beat. "I was in DOJ on 9–11," Barofsky said, "and I saw all my really good FBI agents go over to terrorism. The best agents before who wanted to do complex fraud cases wanted to get Bin Laden."[52]

Additionally, the Justice Department lacked help from other federal agencies that they had in previous crises. Regulatory agencies may have more familiarity with the financial institutions and products at the heart of any potential fraud and can be an important source of support in making a complicated and difficult case. William Black has spoken out about the importance of case referrals from regulatory agencies in building financial fraud cases. Black, a former litigation director of the Federal Home Loan Bank Board and senior deputy chief counsel at the Office of Thrift Supervision (the Bank Board's successor), said during the savings and loan era, his agency filed more than ten thousand referrals to the Justice Department. It also gave Justice attorneys guidance on to how to spot, track, and document financial crimes, resulting in more than a thousand criminal convictions with a success rate of 91 percent.[53] However, Black says in the wake of the 2008 financial crisis, which he categorizes as seven times larger than the savings and loan crisis, federal regulators referred a total of zero cases.[54] Without these case referrals, which would provide a wealth of background information on potentially fraudulent behavior, the risk of a very public loss is higher. An investigative report written about the financial crisis by the U.S. Senate Permanent Subcommittee on Investigations (SPSI) concluded that regulators were too deferential to management in the years leading up to and even after the financial crisis struck. The report details how one regulator, the Office of Thrift Supervision, found many problems at Washington Mutual Bank (WaMu), but continued to merely give recommendations for change, even after previous recommendations were ignored and risk continued to grow. Enforcement action was not even discussed for WaMu until 2008, and even these non-public actions "contained few mandatory measures or deadlines and weren't enough to save the bank."[55]

The underlying question here is why there were no case referrals. There has been a fundamental shift in the federal financial regulatory environment since Black's tenure, he said. As this industry has pushed for increased deregulation, it was able to consolidate its power through major financial mergers made legal by the 1999 repeal of the New Deal-era Glass Steagall Act, which disallowed savings banks and investment banks or insurance companies to operate under the same parent company, as well as disallowing nationwide megabanks to form. Consolidated bank holding companies formed and could in turn use their increased financial and political power to lobby for their own interests. Although basic Depression-era fraud laws remained intact, new financial products that emerged in this period remained unregulated. Credit Default Swaps are an important example of this phenomenon, as they played a major role in the financial crisis, allowing banks to take on increased risk and exposing AIG and others to massive losses.[56]

With less supervision of the sometimes newly created and often poorly understood financial products that were at the heart of the financial crisis, it is no wonder regulators did not refer material for criminal cases to Justice. According to Black, the shift in case referrals came with the Clinton administration and the "New Democrats." Bill Clinton and the Democratic Leadership Coalition (DLC) took a turn away from New Deal Democratic policies that some saw as hostile to the wealthy. It could be categorized as a centrist or right-wing economic turn for the Democratic party that helped it gain Wall Street backers and win back the White House after twelve years of Republican, deregulatory leadership. Black said he left his job as a government regulator when he was told to defer to the bankers and "treat them as our customers."[57] Thomas Frank, in his book, *Listen Liberal*, says the DLC favored upper-class professionalism and abandoned the New Deal economic coalition that supported working-class policies.[58] When viewing bankers as customers, regulators are encouraged to work with them, rather than maintain an adversarial stance. Neil Barofsky also describes the friendly relationship between bankers and regulators during his time in Washington as the Special Inspector General of the bailout fund.[59] While the federal government has a tremendous number of resources at its disposal, one class of defendants can notoriously outspend the government on the best attorneys money can buy—white collar defendants. That is not a new phenomenon. However, as we have seen, the government's massive resource shift within the Justice Department after September 11, 2001 puts it at a further disadvantage against the wealthiest, highest profile defendants in the finance world—executives at major systemically important institutions.

Lastly, prosecutors have had to use these more limited resources to tackle more potential cases. Legal scholar Sara Sun Beale points to an explosion of federal criminal statues since the late 1960s. An American Bar Association study found that more than 40 percent of federal criminal laws passed since the civil war came between 1970 and 1998.[60] "The mismatch between the broad scope of federal criminal law and the relatively narrow scope of federal resources requires federal prosecutors to select a small fraction of cases to prosecute in federal court, leaving the remainder to be prosecuted under state law."[61] White collar defendants often have more resources to battle a government prosecution than street criminals, making these cases that much harder to prosecute in a constrained budgetary environment at the federal level and essentially impossible at the state level, with even less money and resources. Additionally, key federal criminal statutes can be ill-defined, leaving prosecutors with significant room for interpretation. A lack of resources and loosely defined statutes are components of a modern federal law enforcement system that has shifted from an "adversarial trial-focused" one to an "administrative" system. The threat of harsh federal sentences (compared to those at the state level) give prosecutors leverage to make settlements, which is something they have come to rely on as an easier alternative in a resource-limited environment. "In contrast to the traditional expectation that the prosecutor will be subject to multiple checks in an adversarial process that ends in a public jury trial supervised by an independent judge . . . more than ninety percent of all federal convictions are obtained by a guilty plea." Beale points to 2004 as a case in point, during which 83,000 federal defendants' cases were closed but there were only 3,346 federal criminal trials.[62]

The changes in salary differences over the past few decades provides a powerful incentive to behave in a way defense firms would find attractive, namely having a high percentage of wins on high-profile cases. Clients pay top dollar to these defense firms because they believe they are their best chance against a government prosecution, and who better to defend against a government strategy than someone who worked on the inside of a government prosecutor's office. She must be looked upon as the toughest, smartest, and most knowledgeable in what would be a good defense against a prosecution. Because of the Department's own ultra-cautious approach after a series of embarrassments, the defense firms have had to change strategy as well. As the Department relied more upon settlement agreements, defense attorneys with settlement experience would be preferable as well. In the past, when the salary differences were less significant, and the Department itself had not suffered recent high-level embarrassments, government prosecutors could be more aggressive and take on a risky, high-level prosecution. However, by the time the Justice Department attorneys would have had to decide between a prosecution or settlement agreement for the 2008 financial crisis, the risk would not have been worth the potential high-profile loss, especially considering the lack of resources and institutional support for such a case. Indeed, the institutional incentives and personal incentives for prosecutors set the stage for exactly what we received—an overly cautious approach relying on settlements. Without some kind of public report on their investigative efforts—even one that did not disclose specific names to protect the rights of the accused—the public is left wondering why American justice is overly harsh with some and overly lenient with others.

NOTES

1. Whitford, 2002, p. 11.
2. Greenblum, 2005.
3. Moohr, 193.
4. Moohr, pp. 211–215.
5. Barkow, 2013.
6. Barkow, 2013; Wilson.
7. Barkow, 2013, p. 313.
8. Stemen and Federick, 2012.
9. Eisner and Meier, 1990.
10. Eisner and Meier, 1990, p. 269.
11. Baranouski, Ruttenberg, and Stafford Stein, 2014.
12. Department of Justice, Southern District of New York, About, Criminal Division, https://www.justice.gov/usao-sdny/criminal-division.
13. Stewart, 2022.
14. Glasmeier, "Living Wage Calculator—Living Wage Calculation for New York County, New York."
15. Douglas Elliman Real Estate, "Elliman Report—Manhattan, Brooklyn & Queens Rentals."
16. Czajkowski, "$220k Salary Is Needed to Be Happy in NYC: Study."
17. FRED Economic Data.
18. BLS.GOV.
19. Johnson, "Rich and Richer."
20. Department of Justice, Offices of the United States Attorneys, "Administratively Determined Pay Plan Charts," January 11, 2021.
21. Office of Personnel, Pay & Leave Salaries & Wages, Salary Table No. 2014-ES Management.
22. General Schedule, 1985.

23. Priser BLS report, 1985.
24. Harper, "The Lawyer Bubble."
25. Geyelin, "Law-Firm Profits Rose Slightly In 1995 as Hiring Rebounded."
26. Executive & Senior Level Pay Tables (1995), FederalPay.org.
27. Executive & Senior Level Pay Tables (2005), FederalPay.org.
28. Johnson, "Redefining the Super Rich."
29. "Best Law Firms for Criminal Defense White Collar New York."
30. https://www.debevoise.com/andrewceresney?tab=biography.
31. https://www.debevoise.com/andrewceresney?tab=biography.
32. http://www.debevoise.com/professionals/?practice=454013a8-edef-4502-95d5-0bc99ffdf3ee, accessed July 5, 2017.
33. Debevoise.com.
34. https://www.paulweiss.com/professionals/partners-and-counsel/richard-c-tarlowe, accessed March 3, 2018.
35. http://www.paulweiss.com/professionals.
36. http://www.cadwalader.com/professionals/jodi-avergun, accessed July 5, 2017.
37. https://www.pbwt.com/white-collar-defense-and-investigations/, accessed July 5, 2017.
38. https://www.davispolk.com/professionals/greg-andres/, accessed July 5, 2017.
39. https://www.davispolk.com/professionals/denis-mcinerney/, accessed July 5, 2017.
40. https://www.ropesgray.com/biographies/m/michael-g-mcgovern.aspx, accessed July 5, 2017.
41. https://www.ropesgray.com/biographies/l/joshua-s-levy.aspx, accessed July 5, 2017.
42. https://www.paulweiss.com/professionals/partners-and-counsel/adam-b-schwartz, accessed July 1, 2018
43. https://www.debevoise.com/davidsarratt?tab=biography, accessed July 3, 2018.
44. Rakoff interview.
45. OIG Report, September 2005.
46. Holland, September 17, 2013.
47. Lichtblau et al., 2008.
48. Lichtblau et al., 2008.
49. Lichtblau et al., 2008.
50. FCIC, 2011, p. 163.
51. FCIC, 2011, p. 163.
52. Barofsky interview.
53. Black interview, Calavita et al., 1997.
54. Black interview.
55. SPSI report, 2011, p. 209.
56. See earlier discussion of AIG Financial Products CEO Cassano for further details.
57. Black interview.
58. Frank, *Listen Liberal*.
59. Barofsky, *Bailout*.

60. Beale, 2009, p. 399.
61. Beale, 2009, p. 400.
62. Beale, 2009, p. 401.

Chapter 8

Alternative Explanations

MONEY IN POLITICS

Perhaps the most popular explanation for why no major executives were criminally prosecuted for the 2008 financial crisis is the idea that they simply are too powerful to jail because they give a lot of money to politicians. This is a tempting theory considering how powerful the finance industry had become by the end of the twentieth century. There are pros and cons to this theory.

In the twenty-five years preceding the 2008 financial crisis, the financial services industry grew from 5 percent to 8 percent of gross domestic product (GDP), growing 60 percent faster than the economy itself, as part of the country's late twentieth century move from an industrial economy to a service-based one.[1] Additionally, individual compensation grew dramatically in the financial services industry, when investment banks went from private partnership to public companies in the 1980s and 1990s. By 2005, financial sector executive pay was the highest of any industry, averaging \$3.4 million per year.[2] The finance industry's contribution total to federal candidates increased dramatically from \$70 million in 1990 to \$518 million in 2008 and \$677 million in 2012. Adjusted for inflation, this is still a big increase, with \$70 million in 1990 equating to \$122.97 million in 2012 dollars.[3] Lobbying efforts have also increased with the industry having spent \$200 million in 1998 (\$264 million in 2008 dollars[4]) and close to \$500 million each year since 2008.[5]

> Former Securities and Exchange Commission chairman Arthur Levitt told the (Financial Crisis Inquiry Commission) that once word of a proposed regulation got out, industry lobbyists would rush to complain to members of the congressional committee with jurisdiction over the financial activity at issue. According to Levitt, these members would then "harass the SEC with frequent letters

> demanding answers to complex questions and appearances of officials before Congress. These requests consumed much of the agency's time and discouraged it from making regulations.[6]

The idea that an interest group would hold significant sway over lawmakers and policy makers is known as regulatory capture. Carpenter and Moss define regulatory capture as "the result or process by which regulation, in law or application, is consistently or repeatedly directed away from the public interest and toward the interests of the regulated industry, by the intent and action of the industry itself."[7] Regulatory capture can result in less regulation to protect consumers or more regulation that favors some businesses over others. Utilities, trucking companies and rail roads have often been examples of industries benefiting from either deregulation or regulation favoring a particular firm or industry over others.[8] John M. de Figueiredo and Brian Kelleher Richter argue lobbying has a greater impact than direct campaign donations, with its spending exceeding campaign contributions fivefold.[9] They define lobbying as "the transfer of information in private meetings and venues between interest groups and politicians, their staffs, and agents."[10] Lobbying by corporations and trade associations account for approximately 85 percent of lobbying spending on both the federal and state level. Additionally, larger corporate groups are much more likely to lobby than smaller interests.[11]

Any discussion of regulatory capture is incomplete without mentioning political scientist E. E., Schattschneider's classic work *The Semisovereign People*. It says that the Madisonian pluralist ideal of factions checking each other is inaccurate, as wealthier interests have inherent advantages and will capture government officials in a transaction or consumer-like approach.[12] The idea that Wall Street firms and executives' campaign donations have influence over lawmakers is no exception to this story. However, some political science studies fail to find measurable direct influence.[13] Other authors point not to direct influence, but to the agenda-setting power of interest groups to control what is and is not considered in the legislative arena.[14] Public administration scholar David Lowery challenges the traditional literature's frequent historical conclusion that a connection between lobbying and policy outcomes cannot be found. He redefines the concept of influence and argues for a more inclusive methodology, claiming the focus on observable and measurable results may overproduce null results and miss important factors. In fact, influence may exist, but it is difficult to directly measure. Influence in all its forms is complex and diffuse, and the nature of academic research is to focus on direct effects, "narrowly observed."[15] Simply because influence may be difficult to measure, does not mean we should discount it.[16] Indirect influence is particularly relevant to the Justice Department, as there is no opportunity for interest groups to provide money to career prosecutors, but budgetary influence and campaign finance promises to political appointees for future campaigns offer opportunity for capture.

Political economist Ernesto Dal Bo argues that capture is possible due to the information advantages industries have over the diffuse concept of the public. Citizens are likely not knowledgeable about the relevant issues or even aware that policy is being considered. If government regulators are not lured to the private sector with exponentially higher wages and they are constantly monitored in their decision-making process, they may be less likely to make decisions that favor narrow interest groups over best practices or the public interest. However, Dal Bo finds this impractical alone and suggests institutional remedies, such as information sharing, legislative oversight and support for consumer groups. He does note that they are already in place to varying regional degrees in the United States.[17] Additionally, interest groups may capture regulators by providing an abundance of information that plays in their favor and encouraging regulators who lack the time to research alternative views thoroughly to share their worldview.

Perhaps more relevant to the regulators whom Black described in the previous chapter as thinking of the finance industry as their clients than to Justice Department attorneys, Dal Bo advocates for finding optimal term lengths for government regulators, as overly long tenures allow collusion with a firm and too short a time makes regulators fear "rocking the boat" too close to the time when they may seek a job with the industry. Elected regulators tend to have a more pro-consumer stance, as they are more responsive to popular will, he says. However, the public may not be able to discern their own self-interest when there is an information imbalance. Regulators with an industry background tend to be more lenient to industry, but "not particularly so" when controlling for party affiliation. The promise of an industry job only tended to impact leniency when the regulator's tenure is almost over.[18]

Hall and Wayman showed in 1990 that interest groups and individuals do receive something for their money: time. This access can be helpful in lobbying lawmakers on what types of legislation they should support, how they conduct oversight of agencies and even what language to use when writing legislation. Especially when focused at the committee level, political donations and lobbying money may not buy votes or influence elections directly, so much as buy extremely valuable time and attention from an elected official. Giving money to politicians who sit on the relevant committee makes the money work harder, as it targets lawmakers who have the keenest interest in the issue at hand and therefore likely to be sympathetic to the interest group. Additionally, the committee level provides a less formal environment with less public scrutiny that floor votes. Therefore, politicians can respond to monied interests more safely at this stage in the lawmaking process.[19]

In 2002, economist Thomas Stratmann sought to discover whether money influences votes or interest-group friendly lawmakers attract donations with their votes. In other words, in what direction does the arrow of causation point? He studied voting behavior of Congressmembers on key pieces of legislation in 1991 and 1998 that sought to dismantle the financial regulations set out in Glass Steagall. He found that higher contributions led to a higher probability of a lawmaker voting in the group's interests, as well as against an opposing group's interests.[20] University of Kansas researchers in 2009 found a useful empirical measure for lobbying efficacy by measuring the amount of money spent influencing the American Jobs Creation Act of 2004. This bill allowed multinational corporations to repatriate earnings for a one-time lower tax rate. With these companies subject to public disclosures, the researchers could compare the company's savings achieved in that single tax year to the amount it spent to push for the policy, providing a unique opportunity to measure the effect of lobbying. Indeed, the researchers found the companies on average gained $220 for every $1 spent lobbying lawmakers regarding this Act, for a 22,000 percent return on their investment.[21] Lastly, common sense dictates that companies and groups spend money on lobbying because it gets them something beneficial in return.

However, an increase in finance industry spending on campaign donations and lobbying from one crisis to the next does not necessarily mean it can describe the change in prosecutorial behavior. Indeed, Calavita, Pontell, and Tillman argue that political connections and donations were at the heart of the savings and loan (also known as thrift) crisis of the 1980s and 1990s, after which hundreds of executives went to prison. They quote Federal Home Loan Bank Board Chairman Edwin J. Gray as saying "The thrift crisis is, and has been from the beginning, a political crisis."[22] More than 160 political action committees (PACs) represented the savings and loan industry in the years leading up to the peak of the crisis and actually ramped up contributions significantly as the worst of the crisis approached. Between 1983 and 1988, these PACs gave $4.5 million in campaign contributions for House and Senate races and $1 million for individual members of the banking committee. In total, estimates show the industry is responsible for approximately $12 million in political contributions to federal candidates and political parties during the 1980s.[23] At the time the financial industry was also the largest donor for politicians giving speeches, known as "honoraria," which was regulated as personal income, not campaign finance. The Reagan administration and congressional Republicans at the time were certainly ideologically on board with the deregulation that benefited savings and loan banks and ultimately contributed to the crisis. But Calavita, Pontell, and Tillman argue that the politically influential industry played a major role in shaping the details of that deregulation.[24] House Banking Committee Chairman Congressman

Fernand St. Germain had called in the 1970s for greater uniformity in regulations after the failure of Citizens State Bank due to the actions of "fraudulent insiders and affiliated outsiders."[25] By the early 1980s, St. Germain had co-sponsored two major pieces of legislation that phased out important regulations. Unsurprisingly, this change of heart was connected with his "increasingly cozy relationship" with the U.S. League of Savings Institutions, one of the most powerful Washington lobbyists at the time.[26]

> St. Germain was a regular recipient of the League's largesse in the early 1980s as thrift deregulation was being considered. In fact, one of the League's main lobbyists, James "Snake" Freeman, was assigned the task of taking the House Banking Committee Chairman out on the town on a regular basis. Having been observed frequently dining out in Washington on the League's expense account and in the company of the League's lobbyist. St. Germain was investigated by the U.S. Department of Justice for conflict-of-interest violations. The Justice Department concluded that there was "substantial evidence of serious and sustained misconduct" by St. Germain in his connections with the third industry. A House Ethics Committee investigation came to the same conclusion. However, no formal prosecution was initiated, and St. Germain was vote out of office in 1988.[27]

However, we must not forget that this discussion is about prosecution by government lawyers, not policies or laws made by politicians. Lobbyists focus their attention on lawmaking and rulemaking, not prosecutorial efforts. There are many groups that lobby the Department of Justice.[28] Indeed, anyone can "lobby" the Department in the sense that they can visit Regulations.gov, search for open proposed regulations posted by the Department and type in their thoughts. However, lobbying the Department means weighing in on publicly available proposed rulemaking like all agencies offer, as required to by law, unless it is a national security matter. It does not mean weighing in on whom to prosecute. Indeed, a prosecutor's deliberations and decision making are not public matters, whereas lawmaking and rulemaking is both public and multi-staged, providing ample access points for lobbyists or citizen comment.

Lobbying and campaign donations can cause capture for regulators, but it applies less to prosecutors because of the secretive nature of their process. To be sure, wealthy people can afford the best attorneys to negotiate with government prosecutors even before any charges would be filed and this has myriad benefits. Lobbyist for powerful industries can influence regulators who would have contributed case referrals and weaken the laws themselves.

A general sense of political influence by monied interests is a popular explanation for why Wall Street executives didn't face prosecution for the 2008 crisis. However, this narrative falls short when examined more closely. As described in this chapter, monied interests worked their will on the political system in the late 1980s and early 1990s when the savings and loan crisis saw hundreds of bank executives criminally prosecuted. Powerful executives in had influence over politicians in the early 2000s as well, when company executives like Enron's Chairman Kenneth Lay were successfully prosecuted for their corporate crimes. (Lay and others will be further detailed in a subsequent chapter.) Additionally, lobbyists do not have access to the prosecutorial decision-making process like they do to the public and multi-access point lawmaking and regulatory processes. Therefore, despite the popularity of this explanation, it ultimately fails as a satisfying answer at this time as capture and political influence have been consistent factors across financial crises of recent decades and lobbying pressure is removed from the secretive process of prosecutorial discretion.

NOTES

1. FCIC, 2011, p. 64.
2. FCIC, 2011, p. 63.
3. https://www.in2013dollars.com/us/inflation/1990?endYear=2012&amount=70.
4. https://www.in2013dollars.com/us/inflation/1998?endYear=2008&amount=200.
5. Opensecrets.org.
6. FCIC Report, p. 53.
7. Carpenter and Moss, p. 13.
8. Dal Bo, pp. 206, 207.
9. de Figueiredo and Richter, 2013.
10. de Figueiredo and Richter, 2013.
11. de Figueiredo and Richter, 2013.
12. Schattschneider, 1960.
13. Dahl 1961; Baumgartner and Leech, 1998.
14. Baumgartner and Jones, 1993
15. Lowery, 2013.
16. Bachrach and Baratz, 1962; Dahl, 1961.
17. Dal Bo, 2006, p. 221.
18. Dal Bo, 2006.
19. Hall & Wayman, 1990.
20. Stratmann, pp. 15–16.
21. Alexander et al., 2009.
22. Calavita et al., 1997, p. 86.
23. Calavita et al., 1997, p. 87.
24. Calavita et al., 1997, pp. 88–89.
25. Calavita et al., 1997, 89.
26. Calavita et al., 1997, 90.
27. Calavita et al, 1997, 91.
28. Opensecrets.org.

Chapter 9

Alternative Explanations

PRESIDENTIAL LEADERSHIP STYLE

To understand whether presidential leadership style could explain why executives were prosecuted during earlier crises and not in 2008, the role of the president must be examined across these events. The relevant presidents for this discussion are George H. W. Bush, George W. Bush and Barack Obama. When considering the 2008 crisis, President Obama is the only player I will consider. President George W. Bush left office while the crisis was still raging, and he and his administration were focused on the immediate danger. George W. Bush, however, was in office when prominent executives were criminally prosecuted for the accounting scandals in the early 2000s, and his father George H. W. Bush held the presidency when many cases were filed during the savings and loan crisis. While presidential leadership is another attractive popular theory, has challenges considering a few factors, such as the norm of prosecutorial independence from the political process. To be sure, the president appoints the most senior leadership of the Justice Department, including the Attorney General and the United States Attorneys. A president can and does appoint like-minded individuals to lead these offices. This chapter will explore how much influence the President can have on federal criminal prosecutions. It should be noted that Congress could also be examined as a factor for this study. Congress's relevancy here would be in allocating the federal budget, including that of the Justice Department. I ultimately declined to include Congress, as it is one step further removed from the decision-making process than the president and therefore outside the scope of this inquiry, but could be explored in future work.

HOW PRESIDENTS INFLUENCE

As the head of the Executive Branch, which houses the Justice Department, the primary ways that a president would have influenced the decision to prosecute would be through appointees, allocation of existing resources and rhetorical pressure. How much do these influences matter? The Justice Department is ostensibly the most apolitical of all government actors, along with the judiciary. Fordham University Law School Chair Bruce A. Green and New York Law School Professor Rebecca Roiphe call prosecutorial independence "the cornerstone of American democracy," in a 2018 research article. The presidencies of Richard Nixon and Donald J. Trump put this idea to the test. While Nixon fired Attorneys General until he found one that would act according to his wishes, but did not explicitly claim he could order the Justice Department to make specific decisions, Trump has done both.[1] He directly called for his political enemies to be prosecuted innumerable times and claimed that he has absolute control over the Justice Department.

Donald Trump's behavior sparked a nation-wide discussion on what presidents can do legally and what expectations are simply norms. Trump sparked a conversation around what a president could or could not do. Americans quickly realized that many things thought impossible for a president, like interfering in criminal prosecutions, were simply norms and traditions, which could be broken. Trump has certainly broken through those norms in many ways, such as with his attempts to call for his political enemies to be criminally investigated and prosecuted and finding an attorney general, Bill Barr, who will do his best to be Trump's political ally. For example, Barr's Justice Department filed a motion to withdraw the criminal case against former National Security Adviser Michael Flynn. Jonathan Stevenson, a Senior Fellow at the International Institute for Strategic Studies and a former National Security Council Director for Political-Military Affairs, Middle East and Africa from 2010 to 2013, wrote in the *New York Review of Books* that this move is unprecedented for the Justice Department because it came after Flynn already plead guilty more than two years prior for lying to the FBI regarding his involvement with Russian interference in the 2016 election.[2]

> Such motions are extremely rare to begin with, and after guilty pleas they are unprecedented. This particular motion is also a freakish document that distorts the law and misrepresents the views of former senior Justice Department officials involved in the Flynn case.[3]

Trump made it clear that although he hadn't had much success in jailing those that threatened his power, he could get his allies out of jail and make other unprecedented legal moves. However, Trump's use of the Justice Department in this way only had the support of a few of the most loyal members of his inner circle, like Barr. His previous Attorney General, Jeff Sessions, despite being a solidly Republican partisan, ultimately refused to bend justice to Trump's will. He was subsequently forced to resign as Attorney General in November 2018 when he recused himself from investigating the Russian interference of the 2016 campaign, of which he was an active member.[4] Despite his intense loyalty to Trump, Sessions ultimately put the rule of law over partisanship in this instance. This example echoes Green and Roiphe's argument that the professional norms instilled in the minds of all lawyers help make it possible for Justice Department norms of prosecutorial independence to be largely upheld, despite the few Trump loyalists that do his bidding at Justice. "In order to ensure democratic accountability, the President's legitimate policy agenda may shape prosecutorial priorities, but partisan politics and personal interest must play no role in determining the course of individual cases."[5]

They and other scholars argue that there is abundant evidence against a true all-powerful executive, but more of a complicated web of departments checking each other within the Executive Branch. In addition to the long-established rule-of-law norms instilled in all lawyers during school and training, the Constitution can be referenced to assess the president's power over the Justice Department. While it doesn't specifically prevent the president from directing the Justice Department, it also does not permit him to do so. It ultimately gives Congress the power to determine whether a president can interfere in specific prosecutorial decisions rather than setting general policy and appointing leaders.[6] However, Congress and the president have battled since the country's founding over control of the bureaucracy. Scholars debate the issue, while presidents and Congressional leaders put theories to the test with specific actions that push the boundaries and in the process shape norms. Therefore, it is a de facto ongoing conversation about who controls the Justice Department. Meanwhile, it continues to remain one of the most independent parts of the bureaucracy.

Moving on from direct orders, I will examine the softer powers a president may use to control prosecutions. Barack Obama took office in January 2009, also preoccupied with easing the crisis and stabilizing the economy. However, by the end of 2009 the recession was over and the economy was growing again. This was the time when he could have focused on correcting the ills that caused the crisis. Indeed, his administration did focus extensively on passing the Dodd-Frank financial reform law in 2010. Additionally, he was responsible for setting the rhetoric during this time. Would he set a tone of a sheriff going after lawbreakers or a negotiator trying to find resolution? He brought at group of thirteen major bank leaders into his White House to discuss the crisis. He told them that he and his White House were the only thing standing between them and "the pitchforks." He would be the negotiator, the peacemaker and the healer. Certainly, he did not take on a tone of "sheriff," looking to round up lawbreakers and bring them to justice. This approach could explain an abundance of settlement agreements over prosecutions, which is what occurred after the 2008 crisis. In comparison, prosecutions for the savings and loan and accounting scandal crises under the George H. W. Bush and George W. Bush administrations respectively may be surprising for such business-friendly administrations.

It is possible that the Bush presidents focused more on law enforcement rather than new regulation, such as the Dodd-Frank law of 2010 pushed by the Obama administration. However, both Bush administrations did see new high-profile laws like the Financial Institutions Reform, Recovery, and Enforcement Act of 1989 and the Bipartisan Campaign Reform Act of 2002, otherwise known as McCain-Feingold, in addition to criminal prosecutions. Another possible explanation is that the notoriously business-friendly Bush administrations had to prosecute these cases, lest they look unwilling to hold their own friends accountable and lose support from those who seek to keep the power of corporations in check. Conversely, President Obama was thought of as left-leaning or liberal and therefore may not have wanted to appear too harsh on corporations. The Obama administration also had to handle the optics of the first black presidency in a racist society, which would have posed a variety of challenges. He entered office with much political capital based on an electorate wanting "hope" and "change." Obama's political capital was essentially spent on the Affordable Care Act (known as Obamacare), the $787 billion American Recovery and Reinvestment Act of 2009 (known as the stimulus), and the Dodd-Frank Wall Street Reform and Consumer Protection Act of 2010,[7] not encouraging white collar criminal enforcement.

Certainly, President Obama may be described as assertive in many ways. Indeed, for a person to win election to the presidency of the United States, let alone to accomplish this twice, he must be intensely driven. However, it seems to be part of Obama's personality style to seek compromise, rather than battle. Similarly, the Obama Justice Department's approach to white collar crime, specifically, may be one example of that "negotiator" approach. Political scientist Stanley Renshon's model of presidential analysis takes a psychological approach, "focused on three core elements—found in everyone, not just presidents—ambition, character integrity (ideals and values), relationships with others (relatedness), and their relationship to political leadership and decision making, the latter two being the twin cores of presidential responsibility."[8] According to Renshon, Obama saw the failed ambitions of his father and grandfather, leading him to aim high with his own ambitions. He carried a sense of moral leadership, justice. and fairness from his mother, who also worked for these types of changes in Indonesian villages. These relationships influenced who the adult Obama would become. The roots of his deliberate and careful nature may be found in his relationship with his mother, who has been described as impulsive and reckless. She and Obama's father did not know each other well when they married and had a child. After Obama's father abandoned the family and moved back to his native Africa with another woman, his mother married another man and moved the family to Indonesia, a country that was foreign to her and had recently experienced a bloody coup. She also left Obama with his grandparents for a time to work on field research. Renshon points to this recklessness as "impacting his determined deliberativeness."[9] Obama is known for his cool, calm and rational persona and as a pragmatist. Renshon focuses on Obama's assertive progressive agenda on health care and alternative energy, despite his pragmatism.[10] These may be examples of his focus on social justice; however, it should be noted that the Obama administration did attempt to include Republicans and others in these efforts.[11] More importantly for this study, it is Obama's tendency to be cautious, perhaps overly so to compensate for the recklessness of his parents. This overly cautious tendency may help explain why he did not aggressively push for punishment of financial crisis-era executives.

It is reasonable to assume that a president would appoint like-minded individuals to his cabinet, which includes the Attorney General. Then the Attorney General can direct the Justice Department. Indeed, some have said the Department suffered from an overabundance of caution during the tenure of Eric H Holder Jr. (2009–2015)[12] "I think the Holder Justice Department was very risk averse," said Neil Barofsky, former Special Inspector General for the Troubled Asset Relief Program (otherwise known as the "bailout") and a former Southern District of New York prosecutor. During previous crises, the administration created a task force, made of up members from various relevant federal agencies, to coordinate enforcement efforts. Those earlier task forces were taken much more seriously than the one established by President Obama in 2009.[13] "The Obama task force did nothing. I am told by people on the task force that they weren't asked to do anything. If not for political pressure, they wouldn't have done what they did (civil settlements). They kept upping the fines—that's just the cost of doing business," according to a knowledgeable source.[14]

President Obama may have feared "spooking" the fragile recovering market by looking "too tough" on the banks into which it had just poured massive federal resources. On the other hand, if criminal charges had been brought after the crisis had ebbed—the statute of limitations was five years for some charges and ten for others—perhaps this negative impact would no longer have been an issue.[15] Additionally, cases against individuals could be framed as brought against "bad actors" rather than institutions as a whole. Although the longer they waited, the harder it would have been to make the case, as memories of potential witnesses would have faded and some evidence might have been lost, Barofsky said. Previous administrations took the stance that charging individuals was an important component of corporate law enforcement. Indeed, a memo written by George W. Bush administration Assistant Attorney General Mark Filip on August 28, 2008, calls for individuals to face prosecution for corporate crimes.

> Because a corporation can act only through individuals, imposition of individual criminal liability may provide the strongest deterrent against future corporate wrongdoing . . . Only rarely should provable individual culpability not be pursued, particularly if it relates to high-level corporate officers, even in the face of an offer of a corporate guilty plea or some other disposition of the charges against the corporation.[16]

HOW PRESIDENTS ARE INFLUENCED

We have discussed what influence presidents have on prosecutions, but what influences their decision-making? Presidents are influenced by a variety of factors, including advisors, political party leaders, voters and Congressmembers. Perhaps the most popular explanation for what motivates any elected official is money. Indeed, money to run a successful election or reelection campaign is essential. Voters want to get to know the candidates personally and pricey television ads are still a popular tool in the internet age. Therefore, politicians need funding. Specifically, it is easy to see how important the finance industry is to presidential campaigns. In the 2004 presidential election, the list of the top five largest donors to both the George W. Bush campaign and John Kerry's campaign include financial services companies. John Kerry's fourth and fifth largest donors were Goldman Sachs ($314,000) and Citigroup Inc. ($300,325), respectively. All five of Bush's top donors were financial services companies.[17]

Financial services companies contributing large sums of money to presidential campaigns, especially the business-friendly George W. Bush, does not come as a surprise. However, the industry's donation patterns in 2008 may have been unexpected. Republican candidate John McCain's top five donor list includes more financial service companies than his opponent, Democrat Barak Obama, but in terms of dollar amounts, the financial services businesses gave more to Obama.[18] The finance industry gave $43,744,789 to Obama compared to $31,043,978 to McCain.[19]

Do these large campaign donations from the financial elite explain why the Obama Administration declined to prosecute them? This is certainly a common refrain heard among the lay public, but it falls short as an explanation because presidents have taken money for their campaigns from financial services companies across the crises in question. To be sure, logic dictates that it would be difficult to aggressively prosecute people responsible for hundreds of thousands or millions of dollars in campaign support. However, this theory is ultimately not compelling because of the distance between the president and federal prosecutorial decision making. Additionally, prosecution of major political benefactors in previous crises also makes the argument weak.

The starkest example of the flaw in the idea that campaign donations bought a get out of jail free card is Kenneth Lay, the founder and chairman of Enron Corporation. Lay, nicknamed "Kenny Boy" by President George W. Bush, had given more than $550,000 to Bush's campaigns for governor and president over the years of their friendship back in Texas. Not only was Lay a major donor for Bush, but both men agreed on major policy areas, such as energy market deregulation. Lay also helped to fundraise for Bush's father, President George H. W. Bush, and helped to bring the Bush Presidential Library to Houston. Yet, once the accounting fraud scandal within Enron came to light in the early 2000s, the Bush White House sought to distance itself from Lay and the Bush Justice Department created a task force to pursue criminal charges within Enron.[20] Lay was ultimately convicted in May 2006 of six counts of fraud and conspiracy, with each count carrying a maximum sentence of five to ten years jail time. However, he died in July 2006 at his home in Aspen, Colorado at the age of 64 before the court handed down a sentence, which was scheduled for the fall of that year. He had been free on a $5 million bond.[21]

Although I have found little concrete reason to believe presidential influence is a major factor in prosecutorial discretion, this chapter certainly does not offer a complete exploration of the topic. Presidential leadership style and influence over prosecutorial decision-making has much potential for further inquiry, particularly in light of the way the Trump presidency challenged the very rule of law itself.

NOTES

1. Green and Roiphe, 2018.
2. Stevenson, "With Flynn, Barr Burns Justice to Feed Trump's 'Obamagate' Fantasy."
3. Stevenson, "With Flynn, Barr Burns Justice to Feed Trump's 'Obamagate' Fantasy."
4. Barrett et al., "Jeff Sessions Forced Out as Attorney General."

5. Green and Roiphe, 2018, p. 6.
6. Green and Roiphe, 2018.
7. Suskind, 2011.
8. Renshon 2011, p. 1036.
9. Renshon, 2011, p. 1046.
10. Renshon, 2011.
11. http://www.fels.upenn.edu/recap/posts/negotiation-lessons-passage-aca, accessed August 22, 2017.
12. Eisinger, Rakoff, Barofsky interviews.
13. Black, Rakoff interviews.
14. Interview (anonymous).
15. Rakoff interview.
16. Flilp memo, 2008.
17. Opensecrets.org, Candidate Comparison: Top Contributors 2004 Cycle.
18. Opensecrets.org, Candidate Comparison: Top Contributors 2008 Cycle.
19. Opensecrets.org, Candidate Comparison: Top Contributors 2004 Cycle.
20. Oppel Jr. and Van Natta Jr., "Enron's Collapse: The Relationships; Bush and Democrats Disputing Ties to Enron."
21. Peters and Romero, 2006. "Enron Founder Dies before Sentencing."

Chapter 10

Alternative Explanations

CULTURAL CAPTURE

Cultural capture is different from traditional capture in the sense that it is emotional and mental processes that make a regulator favor someone, rather than direct or future monetary gain. Cultural capture has three components; in-group preferencing—the idea that people in the same social and cultural circles tend to favor each other; status—admiring and treating preferentially those who are perceived to be elevated within a social hierarchy; and social connections—treating preferentially those with whom we have social connections. When making decisions, humans in general are largely "irrational" beings—or imperfect calculators of all information and all possible outcomes.[1] In fact, an understanding of cognitive biases can shed light on how people make decisions with imperfect information.[2] Legal scholar James Kwak provides a compelling narrative for cultural capture in his book *13 Bankers*, but he ultimately also acknowledges the difficulty in proving cultural identity and its influence on a person's decision making.[3] Kwak argues that the status of financial services people rose in the decades leading up to the financial crisis, as banks used increasingly complicated mathematical and computer models in trading, necessitating and attracting employees from elite universities. Kwak points to this as a reason to take the potential resultant cultural capture into consideration in explaining the financial crisis of 2008, because it may have prevented regulators from taking a firm approach with industry.[4]

Law professor Alafair S. Burke examined how cognitive bias impacts prosecutorial decision-making using a racially tinged rape and murder case, in which DNA evidence exonerated a convicted mentally impaired Black farmhand, but prosecutors continued to insist he remained a viable suspect.[5] While prosecutors may exhibit confirmation against the innocence of a mentally impaired Black man accused of raping and murdering a White woman, they may exhibit other biases that work in favor of other educated, professional people (usually men)—like themselves—in the world of finance.[6] Imagine prosecutors and Wall Street executives in a room together. They all look like middle- or upper-class people. They might all be white. Whether or not their clothes and grooming cost a lot of money, or just look smart for the price, they are all dressed in a suit and are clean cut. They look like they belong in a room together. On the other hand, a "common street criminal" may appear very different from a prosecutor. They would be dressed more casually and may have vastly different hairstyles, body adornment, speech patterns, etc. They appear to be adversaries.

While it is reasonable to assume that as humans we are more likely to favor those with whom we identify, and race and gender stereotypes are still pervasive in American life and institutions, it is difficult to gauge what components of a person's identity will motivate them the most. It may be race and gender, as in the case above, or it may be education, social class, race, geographic region, religion, etc. According to Jesse Eisinger, *Pro Publica* reporter and Pulitzer Prize-winning author of a book on the Obama Justice Department called *The Chickenshit Club*, the Obama Justice Department was staffed by those who are educated at more elite institutions and favor the "professional class." "The Obama administration is a bunch of technocrats, beltway establishment Democrats with corporate backers. They are very smart people, very accomplished. They think they are very reasonable. They do not see corporations as malefactors or enemies or systemically rotten," Eisinger said.

Eisinger painted a picture of the well-appointed conference room, in which government prosecutors and defense attorneys for a bank or its executive would meet to discuss a settlement deal.

> No one comes in and blusters and fights and has a lapel that's too wide. No one is making any class faux pas in these meetings. They are all reasonable, calm and smart and give a beautifully detailed PowerPoint presentation about why there hasn't been a crime here, why a settlement would be reasonable, if you really want to go for something and why you're going to lose in court. It all comes across at the time very reasonable.[7]

The idea is to look tough but not unreasonable, and, above all, not to alienate superiors in the Department or prospective defense firm employers. Moreover, as these cases are likely very difficult, their Department superiors may not want to invest in these cases at the expense of relatively simpler cases, Eisinger said. It is also often the case that the young Justice Department or Assistant U.S. Attorneys may be across the negotiating table from their former superiors, who have already made the jump to white-collar defense, adding further social pressure to come to a settlement agreement.[8]

In contrast, the George W. Bush administration began with prosecutors who were more eager to enforce laws aggressively, according to Eisinger. Certainly, the Bush administration could not be called unfriendly to corporations. What was it about these prosecutors that prevented them from identifying with corporate executives? Eisinger explains the change of focus in the Justice Department by looking at the way prosecutors in the Obama administration saw themselves, compared with Bush-era prosecutors. With the later years of the Bush Justice Department plagued by politically motivated U.S. Attorney firings, the Obama Justice appointees saw a need to professionalize the Department, Eisinger said. Eisinger argues the Obama Justice Department heads like Attorney General Eric Holder and Criminal Division Chief Lanny Breuer preferred prosecutors from "big law," who are hesitant to bring aggressive cases.

Holder may be contrasted with Dick Thornburgh, for example, whose Justice Department successfully prosecuted hundreds of executives in the savings and loan crisis. While Holder explained publicly why a criminal prosecution was generally not wise or possible after 2008, Thornburg spoke very differently about the financial executives of his day: "My experience as a United States Attorney and Assistant Attorney General, and as Attorney General teaches that the best way to deter fraud is with tough, timely and effective law enforcement," Thornburgh told the Senate Committee on Banking, Housing, and Urban Affairs on February 9, 1989.[9] The Justice Department during this era prosecuted hundreds of bank executives for the misdeeds of the savings and loan crisis. Did prosecutors really see themselves as more aligned with corporate executives in the Obama years compared to the Bush administrations? Obama-era prosecutors may have seen themselves as more professional, intellectual and reasonable, akin to the corporate executives they negotiated settlement agreements with. They may have even sent their children to the same private schools or were members of the same country club. This could explain why they hesitated to jail those they saw as their "friends" or at least peers. But how do we truly know what these or any other prosecutors felt most important to their identity. Also, identities may be situational and fluctuate over time.

More importantly for this study, the George H. W. Bush and George W. Bush administrations' prosecutors may have been less polished in some ways than Obama-era prosecutors, they hardly excluded Harvard-educated attorneys and clubby relationships with industry executives. A close relationship between regulator and regulated could not be illustrated better than that of George W. Bush and Enron executive Kenneth Lay, whom Bush affectionately referred to as "Kenny Boy." As detailed in a previous section, Lay was also a major contributor to Bush's campaigns. Calavita, Pontell and Tillman write that during the savings and loan crisis, regulators also saw themselves not as foes of the finance industry, but protectors of the economic system. In the case of the savings and loan crisis, regulators saw the crackdown on fraudulent actors in the industry as a way to stabilize the economy.[10] Black, as quoted previously, said that regulators saw their mandates change with the Clinton administration. They had begun to think of the finance industry as their customers. This could explain the difference in approach across crises. Cultural capture, especially as described by Kwak, in an interesting theory. At this time, I find that incentives provide a clearer explanatory picture, but cultural capture may offer some piece of the puzzle. Kwak himself articulated a similar sentiment in a 2013 article on the financial crisis and cultural capture:

> Cultural capture is not a complete explanation of financial regulators' behavior in the run-up to the financial crisis for another reason: the mechanisms that produce cultural capture are basic features of human interactions and therefore predate the recent cycle of financial deregulation.[11]

NOTES

1. Burke, 2006, p.1590.
2. Burke, 2006, p. 1591.
3. Kwak, 2010.
4. Kwak, 2013.
5. Burke, 2006, p. 1587.
6. Burke, 2006, p. 1591.
7. Eisinger interview.
8. Eisinger interview
9. Thornburgh hearing transcript, February 9, 1989.
10. Calavita et al., p. 136.
11. Kwak, 2013.

Conclusion

The answer for one of the most important political questions of our time is not necessarily the most obvious or popular one. It also may not be a simple or single one. This book has sought to explore what makes the most sense given what we do know without being privy to the secretive prosecutorial decision-making process. A popular assumption is that rich people who have connections to government officials through the power of their money can get away with anything. To be sure, there is much reason to think that money influences the political process in many ways. What's more, neither major political party has the monopoly on significant donations and lobbying from the financial services industry.[1] While this concept of regulatory capture of the political process may have had a hand in the weakening of regulations and regulatory enforcement leading up to the crisis, it is a weaker explanation for why no major executives faced jail time afterward. Although the people who run the Justice Department and U.S. Attorney's Offices are appointed by elected officials, they are not elected themselves. In another step further from the political process, the majority of case work is done by career attorneys who are not influenced by campaign donations. Also, lawyers' professional norms and education instill the values of due process and independence from political considerations. Prosecutors often tout their desire to simply "follow the evidence." Even though they are humans who must make choices every day, and therefore can never simply be totally unbiased in the process, they are highly sensitive to criticisms of politicization. The Justice Department clearly shows this desire to look like apolitical and balanced practitioners in the way it responds to outside criticism. Lastly, the connection of political capture to prosecutorial discretion is a weak one because monetary influence in the political process was at work across the savings and loan, Enron-era and 2008 financial crisis eras. However, the influence of powerful industries on lawmaking and rulemaking is an ongoing concern for American democracy.

Presidents are also part of the political process and receive donations from the finance industry. They are subject to lobbying and various other political pressures. They appoint Justice Department leaders with ostensibly similar political leanings. Whether or not they wish to pressure Department leaders for specific prosecutions, it is not so easy for them to do so successfully. Although not directly relevant to the 2008 crisis, Trump's challenge of these prosecutorial independence norms illustrates their existence. He has also stated his frustration over his inability to control the Justice Department.[2] He found in Bill Barr an attorney general willing to act in his interest, but to a much lesser extent than he would have desired, as few others supported these efforts. Leaders within the Justice Department, like the Republican former United States Attorney for the Southern District of New York (2018–2020) Geoffrey Berman, who recently wrote a book about Trump's and Barr's efforts to get the Southern District to prosecute Trump's political enemies and not his allies.[3] "On the eve of (Trump attorney Michael) Cohen's guilty plea, main Justice tried to get our office to remove any reference to Individual-1, who was President Trump. They were unsuccessful in that venture. And they were unsuccessful in every attempt to politically interfere with our office. We held the line in every instance," Berman told ABC's "Good Morning America.[4] Even the highly partisan Jeff Sessions eventually resigned in protest when Trump demanded certain political actions. Ultimately, the role of presidential pressure in prosecutorial decision making could have been an important factor in how aggressively the Justice Department sought to prosecute executives from the 2008 financial crisis, but the connection and explanation was weaker than the personal and institutional incentives faced by prosecutors. It is possible that further research could make an argument for the importance of more presidential involvement, particularly if we see more presidents that seek to wield the power of the Justice Department more expansively, for better or for worse.

Cultural capture is also a compelling theory. It may be intuitive to ask the question: since humans are more likely to give the benefit of the doubt to those with whom they identify and admire, are ivy-league-educated, white-collar attorneys less aggressive in prosecuting white-collar criminals than street criminals? The answer very well may be yes. Cultural capture appears as an explanatory variable in Jesse Eisinger's *Chickenshit Club*, Matt Taibbi's *The Divide*, and James Kwak's *13 Bankers*, but Kwak says this is a difficult theory to prove and says that it needs more study.[5] As Kwak points out, it is at least a potential factor to consider and further explore. Although Eisinger argues that the Obama Justice Department officials saw themselves as educated elites like the increasingly educated elite finance professionals, we cannot know for sure how a prosecutor may see him or herself, and therefore know with whom they identify and admire. Even if he could tell us, would he tell the truth? Would he even really know the truth, or would his unconscious motivations be unknown to him? Also, Wall Street executives are not always seen as consistent entities. Sometimes they are glamorized in novels and films, and sometimes they are vilified. These masters of the universe may have been depicted as smart people who got into a jam, but they also could have been seen as greedy and unethical as well. Therefore, we not only have trouble measuring what prosecutors might truly feel and think, but it is also unclear whether Wall Street executives are figures that they admire, resent or anything in between.

The most compelling narrative explaining why no high-level executives were criminally prosecuted for fraud in the wake of the 2008 financial crisis, in order to most effectively deter future behavior, lies with institutional and personal incentives for Justice Department prosecutors. Winning, high-profile, aggressive prosecutions would be essential for a young prosecutor's career. However, at a time when the Justice Department focused on lucrative settlement agreements rather than seeking jail time, after a series of embarrassments, such as the Arthur Andersen case, a culture of caution encouraged settlements. Why go out on a limb and take the risk—assuming an Assistant United States Attorneys (AUSA) team would even be allowed to do so by their superiors—when the Justice Department's focus was lower-risk, impressive sounding settlement agreements. White-collar defense firms highly value a government prosecutorial a record of success, as evidenced by the kinds of people they hire and how they promote their experience. By the time of the 2008 financial crisis, settlements were de rigueur.

The people given the great power and responsibility of prosecutorial discretion are just that: people. Particularly since these attorneys often live in expensive cities like New York, it would be particularly difficult to expect them not to want a significantly higher salary to pay off law school student loans, support a family, or just enjoy a comfortable living. It is clear that while a lawyer has long been able to earn more money in the private sector, the pay differential between white-collar criminal prosecution and defense has ballooned in the twenty-first century, compared to the latter decades of the twentieth century. There may be many government prosecutors who are dedicated public servants, as Berman described in a September 2022 interview with Jon Stewart.[6] However, even the most ideal among us are motivated by the need to support ourselves and our families, giving them as much as we can. A young, talented Assistant United States Attorney may face six figures in debt from law school, an astronomically high cost of living for a family in New York, and other financial needs and wants. Indeed, Harvard Law School says that most AUSA spend only five to seven years in that position. While a top salary of almost $200,000 is enviable for most people, it is hard to argue with being paid $1 million or more for the same hard work on the other side of the courtroom. Therefore, a smart, talented and hard-working attorney would have a strong incentive to create a resume necessary to obtain this prestigious and lucrative partnership by working on more gettable wins.

As for the institutional incentives of the Department, resource availability is an important factor. It is indeed difficult to make an effective criminal case when Department resources are shifted in large quantities to other priorities. The post–9/11 shift of resources toward terrorism occurred in the years just prior to the 2008 financial crisis, but long after the savings and loan cases were made. Additionally, due to decades of deregulation, regulators coming to see financial companies and leaders as clients, the growing complexity of financial products, and no real money or support for a task force, regulators provided little to no support for successful prosecutions in the form of case referrals, as they had in previous crises. Justice Department and U.S. Attorney's Office leaders would have a hard time putting a team of attorneys on a difficult and high-profile case with this dearth of resources.

All employees respond to the incentives placed before them within the context of the established institutional structures. Although there are many moral and social reasons why one may choose a career, a job's primary purpose is to sustain one's ability to support themselves and those that depend on them. If we expect these human beings to uphold justice as disinterested robots, we are being naïve and unrealistic as a society.

If our goal as a society is to create a Justice Department that upholds and enforces the law in the most even-handed, egalitarian way possible, we must design an institution that incentivizes just that kind of behavior. As it stands, we have incentivized quite the opposite scenario. Pay disparity between the private sector and government service has risen to an unsustainable level. If we wish to incentivize bright and ambitious prosecutors to take on difficult, time-consuming, but nationally important tasks, such as either prosecuting or investigating evidence of widespread and massively damaging fraud that undermines the trust in rule of law that undergirds our democracy, we must give prosecutors the institutional support and financial incentives to do so. Is the solution to pay top government prosecutors $1 million per year to prevent them from moving to the private sector? That very well may be what is needed, or there may be alternative institutional designs that could incentivize these attorneys to act more in the public interest and not shy away from a difficult, but important case. Certainly, that institutional design would have to include incentives to take appropriate risks in the public interest and to provide adequate resources for these types of cases. Regardless, it is unreasonable to expect enough hard-working and ambitious attorneys to take these difficult but important cases out of a sense of moral obligation, overriding an instinctual and powerful need to have a comfortable life for them and their families and without adequate support from superiors and their institution.

A high level of difficulty should not preclude a fair application of criminal justice, but I am not insensitive to the tremendous challenge posed by these cases. Neil Barofsky said that a serious task force should have been well funded and organized by the Justice Department to overcome the challenge of making a successful criminal case. If no charges were warranted, a task force report could have explained this to an angry American public, he said. This would have been a step toward trying to restore faith in the rule of law and justice, regardless of financial status, and may have been a step toward ameliorating some of the populist anger in the years that would follow. Instead, we witnessed the Trump era, with its fascistic undertones, somewhat spurred on by those voters who felt government was not on their side, wherein the move away from rule of law has become even more pronounced. Showing some effort to deeply investigate and report on the public's widespread and persistent suspicion of unpunished criminality on Wall Street, regardless of outcome, would have been worth government resources. In times of major public crisis, such as the Kennedy Assassination, Watergate, and Trump's Russia scandal, independent investigations and subsequent reporting have been warranted, even if no criminal prosecutions resulted. The Financial Crisis Inquiry Commission did a thorough investigation on the regulatory and economic causes of the crisis, and pointed to instances of potential fraud.[7] A similar criminal investigation resulting in either charges filed or a public report to at least give the American public an answer to why no charges were filed in light of these findings, would have been appropriate, as long as the investigation was thorough and as nonpartisan as possible. A well-supported and incentivized Justice Department could certainly have accomplished this task.

Instead, we received vague explanations that seemed more like excuses from the Obama Justice Department, and the public retained a deep sense of unfairness. The 2016 Trump campaign successfully played on this idea that Washington worked only for the rich and powerful, which Trump then parlayed into a norm-busting presidency. The idea that no fraud existed is difficult to take seriously, as one would have to ignore a mountain of potential evidence from civil government cases, settlements and private civil cases, as detailed in earlier chapters. At a time when Democratic norms have been threatened not only by an American president, but by many of his supporters and in his party, it is important to rethink the design of our institutions. In the Madisonian notion that we cannot rely on humans to be angels, so therefore government must be designed to check our worst impulses and foster our best, we must be sure that institutional incentives encourage democratic norms and the rule of law in places like the Justice Department, an important bulwark against those who would have the United States abandon democracy altogether. Although Jon Stewart and former U.S Attorney Geoffrey Berman were talking about Trump's attempt to politicize the Justice Department, to not produce classified documents in response to a subpoena, and "use it as his own law firm," the sentiment also applies to the 2008 crisis as well, when the uber-powerful finance executives were seen to have "gotten away with" crashing the economy without any meaningful punishment and remaining wealthy, while millions of Americans suffered and lost everything. The situation was not the same in 2008 and 2022, to be sure, but the public frustration articulated by Stewart in this interview is the same, and is still a problem for American society. I will give Stewart and Berman the last words:

> Stewart: "I think if you're the public, there's a real frustration that the rule of law doesn't necessarily apply equally."
>
> Berman: "No I get it, and it saw it happen in my experience when Trump, like you said, would use the Department of Justice like his own law firm, target political enemies and benefit political friends, and that eviscerates the rule of law and then people lose faith in the critical institutions of our country, like the Department of Justice, the FBI, the Judiciary, and it's awful. It's destroying the fabric of our country, and we really have to fix it."[8]

NOTES

1. Opensecrets.org.
2. Twitter.com/realdonaldtrump.
3. Stewart, September 2022.
4. Stephanopoulos and Katersky, September 12, 2022.
5. Eisinger, Taibbi, and Kwak.
6. Stewart, September 2022.
7. FCIC Report.
8. Stewart, September 2022.

Bibliography

Abrams, Norman. 2021. "Uncovering the Legislative Histories of the Early Mail Fraud Statutes: The Origin of Federal Auxiliary Crimes Jurisdiction." *Utah Law Review* 2021(5): 1079–1125.

Albonetti, Celesta. May 1991. "An Integration of Theories to Explain Judicial Discretion." *Social Problems* 38(2): 247–266.

Alexander, Raquel Meyer, Stephen W. Mazza, and Susan Scholz. April 8, 2009. "Measuring Rates of Return for Lobbying Expenditures: An Empirical Case Study of Tax Breaks for Multinational Corporations." *Journal of Law and Politics* 25(401): 1–36.

American Bar Association. October 20, 2014. Section 10(b) Litigation: The Current Landscape. https://www.americanbar.org/groups/business_law/publications/blt/2014/10/03_kasner/, accessed October 26, 2021.

Arthur Andersen LLP v. United States, 544 U.S. 696 (2005).

Ashcraft, Adam, Paul Goldsmith-Pinkham, and James Vickery. May 2010. "MBS Ratings and the Mortgage Credit Boom." *Federal Reserve Bank of New York Staff Reports.* no. 449. Federal Reserve Bank of New York.

Bachrach, Peter and Morton S. Baratz. December 1962. "Two Faces of Power." *American Political Science Review* 56(4): 947–952.

Baranouski, Elise, Joan Ruttenberg, and Carolyn Stafford Stein. 2014. "The Fast Track to A U.S. Attorney's Office." Harvard Law School. https://hls.harvard.edu/bernard-koteen-office-of-public-interest-advising/opia-job-search-toolkit/career-and-application-guides/the-fast-track-to-a-u-s-attorneys-office/, accessed September 28, 2022.

Barber, James David. 1972. *The Presidential Character; Predicting Performance in the White House.* Englewood Cliffs, NJ: Prentice Hall.

Barkow, Rachel E. April 2013. "Prosecutorial Administration: Prosecutor Bias and the Department of Justice." *Virginia Law Review* 99(2): 271–342.

Barofsky, Neil. 2013. *Bailout: How Washington Abandoned Main Street While Rescuing Wall Street.* New York: Free Press.

Barofsky, Neil. September 20, 2016. Personal Interview.

Barrett, Devlin, Matt Zapotosky, and Josh Dawsey. November 7, 2018. "Jeff Sessions Forced Out as Attorney General." *Washington Post.* https://www.washingtonpost

.com/world/national-security/attorney-general-jeff-sessions-resigns-at-trumps-request/2018/11/07/d1b7a214-e144-11e8-ab2c-b31dcd53ca6b_story.html, accessed May 16, 2020.

Barrett, Devlin, Sari Horwitz, Robert Costa. March 11, 2017. "New York Federal Prosecutor Preet Bharara Says He Was Fired by Trump Administration." *Washington Post.*

Baumgartner, F. R., and Jones, B. D. 1993. *Agendas and Instability in American Politics*. Chicago: University of Chicago Press.

Baumgartner, F., and Leech, B. 1998. *Basic Interests: The Importance of Groups in Politics and in Political Science*. Princeton, NJ: Princeton University Press.

Beale, Sara S., 2009. "Rethinking the Identity and Role of United States Attorneys." *Ohio State Journal of Criminal Law* 6(2): 369–439.

Beattie, Andrew. June 17, 2022. The Pioneers of Financial Fraud. Investopedia. https://www.investopedia.com/articles/financial-theory/09/history-of-fraud.asp, accessed August 16, 2022.

Bebchukt, Lucian A., Alma Cohentt, and Holger Spamann. 2010. "The Wages of Failure: Executive Compensation at Bear Stearns and Lehman 2000–2008." *Yale Journal on Regulation* 27(2): 257–282.

Berle, A. and Means, G. 1932. *The Modern Corporation and Private Property*. New York: Commerce Clearing House.

"Best Law Firms for Criminal Defense White Collar New York." 2018. *U.S. News & World Report.* https://bestlawfirms.usnews.com/search.aspx?state_code=NY&practice_area_id=41&page=2, accessed February 15, 2018

Bhagat, Sanjai and Brian Bolton. January 2014. "Financial Crisis and Bank Executive Incentive Compensation." *Journal of Corporate Finance* 25: 313–341.

Bharara, Preet. October 23, 2013. S*tatement of Manhattan U.S. Attorney Preet Bharara on the Countrywide, Bank of America, and Rebecca Mairone Verdict.* https://www.justice.gov/usao-sdny/pr/statement-manhattan-us-attorney-preet-bharara-countrywide-bank-america-and-rebecca, accessed October 9, 2017.

Bibas, Stephanos. April 2009. "Prosecutorial Regulation Versus Prosecutorial Accountability." *University of Pennsylvania Law Review* 157(4): 959–1016

Bishop, Keith Paul. September 18, 2007. "The McNulty Memo—Continuing the Disappointment." *Chapman Law Review* 10: 729–744.

Black, William. August 4, 2016. Phone Interview.

Black, William. March 7, 2012. "Prepared Testimony—Examining Lending Discrimination Practices and Foreclosure Abuses." *Senate Committee on the Judiciary.* https://www.judiciary.senate.gov/imo/media/doc/12-3-7BlackTestimony.pdf, accessed July 26, 2021.

Bloomberg News Editorial Board. October 27, 2020. "A Better Approach to Fighting White-Collar Crime." *Bloomberg News.* https://www.bloomberg.com/opinion/articles/2020-10-26/goldman-jpmorgan-cases-there-s-a-better-approach-to-white-collar-crime?srnd=opinion, accessed December 19, 2020.

Borden, Bradley T. and David J. Reiss. March 2013. "Cleaning Up the Financial Crisis of 2008: Prosecutorial Discretion of Prosecutorial Abdication." *Brooklyn Law School Legal Studies Research Papers Accepted Paper Series.* Paper No. 331.

Breslow, Jason M. October 24, 2013. "Bank of America Liable for Mortgage 'Hustle' Program." *Frontline*. http://www.pbs.org/wgbh/frontline/article/bank-of-america-liable-for-mortgage-hustle-program/, accessed October 9, 2017.

Britannica.com. Arthur Andersen. https://www.britannica.com/topic/Arthur-Andersen, accessed August 11, 2022.

Browning, Lynnley. October 27, 2014. "Too Big to Tax: Settlements Are Tax Write-Offs for Banks." *Newsweek.* http://www.newsweek.com/2014/11/07/giant-penalties-are-giant-tax-write-offs-wall-street-279993.html, accessed August 19, 2015.

Buell, Samuel W. 2018. "Why Do Prosecutors Say Anything? The Case of Corporate Crime." *North Carolina Law Review* 96: 823.

Burke, Alafair S. 2006. Improving Prosecutorial Decision Making: Some Lessons of Cognitive Science. *William & Mary Law Review* 47(5): Article 3.

Calavita, Kitty, Henry N. Pontell, Robert H. Tillman. 1997. *Big Money Crime: Fraud and Politics in the Savings & Loan Crisis.* Berkeley: University of California Press.

Carpenter, Daniel and David A. Moss. 2014. *Preventing Regulatory Capture: Special Interest Influence and How to Limit It.* New York: Cambridge University Press.

Cary, Rob. October 28, 2014. "Recalling the Injustice Done to Sen. Ted Stevens." *RollCall.com.* https://www.rollcall.com/2014/10/28/recalling-the-injustice-done-to-sen-ted-stevens-commentary/, accessed October 19, 2021.

Caviness, Elizabeth and Asani Sarkar. August 7, 2020. "Securing Secured Finance: The Term Asset-Backed Securities Loan Facility." Federal Reserve Bank of New York *Liberty Street Economics.* https://libertystreeteconomics.newyorkfed.org/2020/08/securing-secured-finance-the-term-asset-backed-securities-loan-facility.html, accessed July 27, 2021.

Childress, Sarah. January 23, 2013. "DOJ Criminal Chief Lanny Breuer Stepping Down." *PBS.* http://www.pbs.org/wgbh/pages/frontline/business-economy-financial-crisis/untouchables/report-doj-criminal-chief-lanny-breuer-stepping-down/, accessed August 19, 2015.

CNN.com. April 7, 2009. "Sen. Ted Stevens' Conviction Set Aside." http://www.cnn.com/2009/POLITICS/04/07/ted.stevens/, accessed October 19, 2021.

Cohan, William D. September 2015. "How Wall Street's Bankers Stayed Out of Jail." *The Atlantic*. http://www.theatlantic.com/magazine/archive/2015/09/how-wall-streets-bankers-stayed-out-of-jail/399368/, accessed August 20, 2015.

Cohan, William D. February 28, 2017. *Why Wall Street Matters*. New York. Random House Press.

Congressional Budget Office. March 2020. *Report on the Troubled Asset Relief Program.* https://www.cbo.gov/publication/56300, accessed July 26, 2021.

Cornell University Law School. Legal Information Institute. https://www.law.cornell.edu/cfr/text/17/240.10b-5, accessed September 22, 2015.

Crawford, Krysten and Winnie Dunbar. July 8, 2004. "John Rigas Guilty of Conspiracy." *CNN Money.* https://money.cnn.com/2004/07/08/news/midcaps/adelphia_verdict/, accessed October 19, 2021.

Czajkowski, Elise. November 26, 2019. "$220k Salary Is Needed to Be Happy in NYC: Study." *1010 Wins*. https://www.audacy.com/1010wins/articles/news/220k-salary-is-needed-to-be-happy-in-nyc-study, accessed November 25, 2021.

Dahl, R. A. 1961. *Who Governs? Democracy and Power in an American City*. New Haven: Yale University Press.

Dal Bo, Ernesto. July 1, 2006. "Regulatory Capture: A Review." *Oxford Review of Economic Policy* 22(2): 203–225.

Dayen, David. September 25, 2014. "Eric Holder Didn't Send a Single Banker to Jail for the Mortgage Crisis. Is That Justice?" *The Guardian*. http://www.theguardian.com/money/us-money-blog/2014/sep/25/eric-holder-resign-mortgage-abuses-americans, accessed August 19, 2015.

DealBook. November 12, 2009. "Bear Stearns Trial: How the Scapegoats Escaped." *New York Times*. http://dealbook.nytimes.com/2009/11/12/bear-stearns-trial-how-the-scapegoats-escaped/?_r=0, accessed August 18, 2015

DealBook. June 24, 2013. "Rajaratnam Conviction Upheld by Appeals Court." *New York Times*. https://dealbook.nytimes.com/2013/06/24/rajaratnam-conviction-upheld-by-appeals-court/?_r=0, accessed October 26, 2021.

de Figueiredo, John M. and Brian Kelleher Richter. November 2013. "Advancing the Empirical Research on Lobbying." *Annual Review of Political Science* 17: 163–85

de la Merced, Michael J. July 6, 2015. "Eric Holder Returns to Covington & Burling." *New York Times*., accessed August 18, 2015

Dengel, Paul. June 19, 2015. "Second Circuit Rules That FIRREA's Ten-Year Statute of Limitations Applies Even When Banks Participate in the Fraud." *National Law Review*. https://www.natlawreview.com/article/second-circuit-rules-firrea-s-ten-year-statute-limitations-applies-even-when-banks-p, accessed October 5, 2021

Department of Housing and Urban Development. Federal Housing Administration. About Us. https://www.hud.gov/program_offices/housing/fhahistory, accessed August 14, 2022.

Department of Justice Executive Office for United States Attorneys. Fiscal Year 2010. Annual Statistical Report.

Department of Justice, March 14, 2002. News Conference—Arthur Andersen Indictment. https://www.justice.gov/archive/dag/speeches/2002/031402newsconferncearthurandersen.htm, accessed October 19, 2021.

Department of Justice, Office of Professional Responsibility. August 15, 2011. "Investigation of allegations of prosecutorial misconduct in United States v. Theodore F. Stevens, Crim. No. 08–231 (D.D.C. 2009) (EGS)."

Department of Justice, Office of Public Affairs. February 5, 2013. "Department of Justice Sues Standard & Poor's for Fraud in Rating Mortgage-Backed Securities in the Years Leading Up to the Financial Crisis." https://www.justice.gov/opa/pr/department-justice-sues-standard-poor-s-fraud-rating-mortgage-backed-securities-years-leading, accessed November 25, 2021.

Department of Justice, Office of Public Affairs. October 21, 2020. "Justice Department Announces Global Resolution of Criminal and Civil Investigations with Opioid Manufacturer Purdue Pharma and Civil Settlement with Members of the Sackler

Family." https://www.justice.gov/opa/pr/justice-department-announces-global-resolution-criminal-and-civil-investigations-opioid, accessed August 15, 2021

Department of Justice, Offices of the United States Attorneys. January 11, 2021. "Administratively Determined Pay Plan Charts." https://www.justice.gov/usao/career-center/salary-information/administratively-determined-pay-plan-charts, accessed November 25, 2021.

Department of Justice, Southern District of New York. https://www.justice.gov/usao-sdny.

Department of Justice, Southern District of New York. About. Criminal Division. https://www.justice.gov/usao-sdny/criminal-division.

Department of Justice, Southern District of New York. October 23, 2013. "Statement of Manhattan U.S. Attorney Preet Bharara on the Countrywide, Bank of America, and Rebecca Mairone Verdict." https://www.justice.gov/usao-sdny/pr/statement-manhattan-us-attorney-preet-bharara-countrywide-bank-america-and-rebecca, accessed October 26, 2021.

Department of Justice, Southern District of New York. October 20, 2010. "The Future of White Collar Enforcement: A Prosecutor's View Prepared Remarks of U.S. Attorney Preet Bharara New York City Bar Association." https://www.justice.gov/usao-sdny/speech/future-white-collar-enforcement-prosecutor-s-view-prepared-remarks-us-attorney, accessed October 19, 2021.

Douglas Elliman Real Estate. May 2018. "Elliman Report—Manhattan, Brooklyn & Queens Rentals." chrome-extension://efaidnbmnnnibpcajpcglclefindmkaj/viewer.html?pdfurl=https%3A%2F%2Fwww.millersamuel.com%2Ffiles%2F2018%2F06%2FMBQ-May_2018.pdf&clen=392273&chunk=true, accessed November 25, 2021.

Dymski, Gary A., Jesus Hernandez, and Lisa Mohanty. May 2011. "Race, Power, and the Subprime/Foreclosure Crisis: A Mesoanalysis." *Levy Economics Institute.* Annandale-on-Hudson, NY.

Eichengreen, Barry. January 16, 2015. "Financial Crisis: Revisiting the Banking Rules That Died by a Thousand Small Cuts. *Fortune*. http://fortune.com/2015/01/16/financial-crisis-bank-regulation/, accessed January 2015.

Eisinger, Jesse. October 18, 2016. Personal Interview.

Eisner, Marc Allen and Kenneth H. Meier. February 1990. "Presidential Control versus Bureaucratic Power: Explaining the Reagan Revolution in Antitrust." *American Journal of Political Science* 34(1): 269–287.

Eisenstein, James. 1978. *Counsel for the United States: U.S. Attorneys in the Political and Legal Systems.* Baltimore: Johns Hopkins University Press.

Ellis, David. January 11, 2008. "Countrywide Rescue: $4 billion." *CNN Money.* http://money.cnn.com/2008/01/11/news/companies/boa_countrywide/, accessed October 9, 2017.

Fannie Mae. About us. https://www.fanniemae.com/about-us, accessed July 29, 2021

Federal Bureau of Investigation. Enron—Famous Cases & Criminals. https://www.fbi.gov/history/famous-cases/enron, accessed July 25, 2021.

Federal Bureau of Investigation. Financial Crimes Report to the Public Fiscal Years 2010–2011. https://www.fbi.gov/stats-services/publications/financial-crimes-report-2010-2011, accessed October 19, 2021.

Ferguson-Gilbert, Catherine. 2001. "It Is Not Whether You Win or Lose, It Is How You Play the Game: Is the Win-Loss Scorekeeping Mentality Doing Justice for Prosecutors?" *California Western Law Review* 38(1): Article 8.

Flaherty, Anne. June 11, 2019. "BofA CEO Says Government Pressured Bank to Buy Merrill Lynch." *Associated Press.* http://abcnews.go.com/Business/story?id=7818714&page=1, accessed October 9, 2017

Filip, Mark. August 28, 2008. Principles of Federal Prosecution of Business Organizations. (Filip Memo.) U.S. Department of Justice. Office of the Deputy Attorney General.

Financial Sense Wealth Management. September 14, 2011. William Black Transcript. https://www.financialsense.com/contributors/2011/09/14/william-black/transcript, accessed August 6, 2015.

FINRA. *Mortgage-Backed Securities*. https://www.finra.org/investors/learn-to-invest/types-investments/bonds/types-of-bonds/mortgage-backed-securities, accessed July 27, 2021.

Frank, Thomas. 2016. *Listen, Liberal, Or, What Ever Happened to the Party of the People?* New York: Metropolitan Books.

FRED Economic Data. St. Louis Federal Reserve Board. https://fred.stlouisfed.org/series/CPIAUCSL, https://fred.stlouisfed.org/series/CUURA101SEHA.

Frieden, Terry. January 30, 2013. Controversial DOJ Criminal Chief Lanny Breuer Leaving. *CNN*, accessed August 19, 2015 http://www.cnn.com/2013/01/30/politics/lanny-breuer-doj/.

Fox, Justin. April 1, 2010. "What the Founding Fathers Really Thought About. Corporations." *Harvard Business Review*. https://hbr.org/2010/04/what-the-founding-fathers-real.html, accessed October 19, 2021.

Galarza, Daniela. Jan 13, 2016. "Watch Anthony Bourdain Compare Fish to Finance in 'The Big Short.'" *Eater.com*. https://www.eater.com/2016/1/13/10759544/anthony-bourdain-the-big-short-film, accessed November 30, 2021.

Geyelin, Milo. June 18, 1996. "Law-Firm Profits Rose Slightly in 1995 as Hiring Rebounded." *Wall Street Journal.* https://www.wsj.com/articles/SB835927667431628500, accessed September 9, 2021.

Glasmeier, Amy. 2021. "Living Wage Calculator—Living Wage Calculation for New York County, New York." Massachusetts Institute of Technology. https://livingwage.mit.edu/counties/36061, accessed November 25, 2021.

Goldman, David. November 11, 2009. "Former Bear Stearns Execs Not Guilty." *CNN Money.* https://money.cnn.com/2009/11/10/news/companies/bear_stearns_case/, accessed October 5, 2021.

Goldstein, Matthew. June 17, 2016. "Angelo Mozilo Will Not Face Charges for Mortgage Fraud." *New York Times.* https://www.nytimes.com/2016/06/18/business/angelo-mozilo-wil-not-face-us-charges-for-mortgage-fraud.html?_r=0, accessed October 26, 2021.

Gou, Michael, Gary Richardson, Alejandro Komai, and Daniel Park. "Banking Acts of 1932." *Federal Reserve History*. https://www.federalreservehistory.org/essays/banking-acts-of-1932, accessed October 5, 2021.

Gradman, Isaac. November 18, 2016. Phone Interview.

Gramlich, John. June 11, 2019. "Only 2% of Federal Criminal Defendants Go to Trial, and Most Who Do Are Found Guilty." *Pew Research Center*. https://www.pewresearch.org/fact-tank/2019/06/11/only-2-of-federal-criminal-defendants-go-to-trial-and-most-who-do-are-found-guilty/, accessed July 19, 2021.

Green, Bruce A. and Rebecca Roiphe. 2018. "Can the President Control the Department of Justice?" *Alabama Law Review* 70(1). https://ir.lawnet.fordham.edu/faculty_scholarship/932, accessed May 8, 2020.

Greenblum, Benjamin M. October 2005. "What Happens to a Prosecution Deferred? Judicial Oversight of Corporate Deferred Prosecution Agreements." *Columbia Law Review* 105(6): 1863–1904.

Greenspan, Alan. August 17, 2005. "More Capital Is a Less Painful Way to Fix the Banks." *Financial Times*, accessed July 12, 2022.

Greenstein, Fred. 2009. *The Presidential Difference; leadership style from FDR to Barack Obama.* 3rd ed. Princeton, NJ: Princeton University Press.

Investopedia. "What Was the Savings and Loan (S&L) Crisis?" https://www.investopedia.com/terms/s/sl-crisis.asp, accessed July 27, 2022.

Hall, Richard L. and Frank W. Wayman. September 1990. "Buying Time: Moneyed Interests and the Mobilization of Bias in Congressional Committees." *American Political Science Review* 84(3): 797–820.

Hamilton, Colby. October 20, 2014. "In the Eastern District, a Veteran Rises." *Politico.com.* https://www.politico.com/states/new-york/city-hall/story/2014/10/in-the-eastern-district-a-veteran-rises-016695, accessed October 19, 2021.

Harper, Steven J. June 1, 2017. "The Lawyer Bubble." https://thelawyerbubble.com/tag/am-law-100/, accessed July 8, 2017.

Henning, Perter J. December 13, 2010. "The Difficulty of Proving Financial Crimes." *New York Times*. https://dealbook.nytimes.com/2010/12/13/the-difficulty-of-proving-financial-crimes/?_r=0, accessed October 9, 2017

Henriques, Diana. June 30, 2009. "Madoff Is Sentenced to 150 Years for Ponzi Scheme." *New York Times.* https://www.nytimes.com/2009/06/30/business/30madoff.html, accessed October 26, 2021.

Hilt, Eric. September 2008. "When Did Ownership Separate from Control? Corporate Governance in the Early Nineteenth Century." *The Journal of Economic History* 68(3): 645–685.

Ho, Catherine. March 28, 2013. "Lanny Breuer, Chief of DOJ's Criminal Division, Returns to His Old Law Firm Covington & Burling." *Washington Post.* http://www.washingtonpost.com/blogs/capital-business/post/lanny-breuer-chief-of-dojs-criminal-division-returns-to-covington-and-burling/2013/03/27/3b27d7a6-9703-11e2-b68f-dc5c4b47e519_blog.html, accessed August 18, 2015.

Holder, Eric. 1999. "Bringing Criminal Charges against Corporations." (Holder Memo.) U.S. Department of Justice. Office of the Deputy Attorney General.

Holder, Eric. February 5, 2013. Press Release: "Department of Justice Sues Standard & Poor's for Fraud in Rating Mortgage-Backed Securities in the Years Leading Up to the Financial Crisis." U.S. Department of Justice. https://www.justice.gov/opa/pr/department-justice-sues-standard-poor-s-fraud-rating-mortgage-backed-securities-years-leading, accessed October 9, 2017.

Holder, Eric. March 23, 2013. "Sequestration and Safety Actions Regarding the Bureau of Prisons Institutions." U.S. Department of Justice. http://www.justice.gov/sites/default/files/oip/legacy/2014/07/23/sequestration-safety-actions.pdf, accessed October 23, 2015

Holland, Joshua. September 17, 2013. "Hundreds of Wall Street Execs Went to Prison during the Last Fraud-Fueled Bank Crisis." *Moyers on Democracy.* http://billmoyers.com/2013/09/17/hundreds-of-wall-street-execs-went-to-prison-during-the-last-fraud-fueled-bank-crisis/, accessed September 22, 2015.

House of Representatives Financial Services Committee hearing transcript. April 20, 2010. "Public Policy Issues Raised by the Report of the Lehman Bankruptcy Examiner." http://archives-financialservices.house.gov/Hearings/hearingDetails.aspx?NewsID=1080, accessed August 24, 2020.

Irwin, Neil. September 12, 2013. "This Is a Complete List of Wall Street CEOs Prosecuted for Their Role in the Financial Crisis." *Washington Post: Wonkblog.* https://www.washingtonpost.com/news/wonk/wp/2013/09/12/this-is-a-complete-list-of-wall-street-ceos-prosecuted-for-their-role-in-the-financial-crisis/?utm_term=.d2277f1244de, accessed January 5, 2018

Johnson, Chris. May 2015. "Rich and Richer." *American Lawyer Magazine.* https://www.americanlawyer-digital.com/americanlawyer-ipauth/201505ip?pg=122#pg122, accessed September 9, 2021.

Johnson, Chris, May 2017. "Redefining the Super Rich." *American Lawyer Magazine.* https://www.americanlawyer-digital.com/americanlawyer-ipauth/tal201705ip?pg=5#pg5, accessed November 25, 2021.

Justice Department Oversight. March 6, 2013. C-SPAN. http://www.c-span.org/video/?311311-1/justice-department-oversight, accessed August 18, 2015.

Kakutani, Michiko. April 12, 2018. "James Comey Has a Story to Tell. It's Very Persuasive." *New York Times.* https://www.nytimes.com/2018/04/12/books/review/james-comey-a-higher-loyalty.html, accessed July 10, 2018.

Kane, Paul. November 19, 2008. "Sen. Ted Stevens Loses Reelection Bid." *Washington Post.* https://www.washingtonpost.com/wpdyn/content/article/2008/11/18/AR2008111803227.html, accessed October 19, 2021.

Katz, Jack. Winter 1979. "Legality and Equality: Plea Bargaining in the Prosecution of White-Collar and Common Crimes." *Law & Society Review* 13(2): 431–459.

Keefe, Patrick Radden. July 31, 2017. "Why Corrupt Bankers Avoid Jail." *New Yorker*. https://www.newyorker.com/magazine/2017/07/31/why-corrupt-bankers-avoid-jail, accessed January 5, 2018.

Kopan, Tal. March 23, 2017. "DOJ Highlights Immigration Arrests in Statistics Report." *CNN* http://www.cnn.com/2017/03/23/politics/justice-statistics-immigration/index.html. accessed January 17, 2018.

Kreitner, Richard. November 22, 2016. "What Time Is It? Here's What the 2016 Election Tells Us about Obama, Trump, and What Comes Next." *The Nation.* https://www.thenation.com/article/what-time-is-it-heres-what-the-2016-election-tells-us-about-obama-trump-and-what-comes-next/, accessed October 9, 2017

Kroft, Steve. December 12, 2011. "President Obama: The Economy, the Congress, the Future." *CBS News, 60 Minutes.* https://www.cbsnews.com/news/president-obama-the-economy-the-congress-the-future/, accessed July 26, 2021.

Kwak, James and Simon Johnson. 2010. *13 Bankers: The Wall Street Takeover and the Next Financial Meltdown.* New York: Vintage Books.

Kwak, James. 2013. "Cultural Capture and the Financial Crisis." In Daniel Carpenter and David Moss, *Preventing Capture: Special Interest Influence in Legislation, and How to Limit It*, chap. 4. New York: Cambridge University Press.

Lane, Ben. May 23, 2016. "Appeals Court Overturns Bank of America's $1.27 Billion Fine in 'Hustle' Case." *Housing Wire.* https://www.housingwire.com/articles/37092-appeals-court-overturns-bank-of-americas-127-billion-fine-in-hustle-case, accessed October 9, 2017.

Lattman, Peter. December 13, 2006. "The Holder Memo and Its Progeny." *The Wall Street Journal.* http://blogs.wsj.com/law/2006/12/13/the-holder-memo/, accessed January 15, 2016.

Lewis, Neil A. April 1, 2009. "Justice Dept. Moves to Void Stevens Case." *New York Times,* http://www.nytimes.com/2009/04/02/us/politics/02stevens.html, accessed August 18, 2015.

Lichtblau, Eric, David Johnston, and Ron Nixon. October 18, 2008. "F.B.I. Struggles to Handle Financial Fraud Cases." *New York Times.* http://www.nytimes.com/2008/10/19/washington/19fbi.html, accessed 9, 2017.

Lo, Andrew W. June 2015. *The Gordon Gekko Effect: The Role of Culture in the Financial Industry.* NBER Working Paper No. w21267, SSRN: https://ssrn.com/abstract=2618655.

Lowery, David. March 2013. "Lobbying influence: Meaning, Measurement and Missing." *Interest Groups & Advocacy* 2(1): 1–26.

Lowi, Theodore J., 1979. *The End of Liberalism; The Second Republic of the United States.* New York: W.W. Norton & Company.

Massachusetts Institute of Technology Living Wage Calculator. http://livingwage.mit.edu/counties/36061.

Maues, Julia. November 22, 2003. "Banking Act of 1933." *Federal Reserve History.* http://www.federalreservehistory.org/Events/DetailView/25, Accessed August 6, 2015.

McCarthy, Justin. June 16, 2016. "Americans' Confidence in Banks Still Languishing Below 30%." *Gallup News* http://news.gallup.com/poll/192719/americans-confidence-banks-languishing-below.aspx?g_source=position1&g_medium=related&g_campaign=tiles, accessed September 21, 2017.

McCleskey v. Kemp, 481 U.S. 279, 297, 312 (1987), (quoting Kenneth Culp Davis, Discretionary Justice 170 (1969)).

Meares, Tracy L. 1995. "Rewards for Good Behavior: Influencing Prosecutorial Discretion and Conduct with Financial Incentives." *Fordham Law Review* 64(3): 851.

Mears, Bill. May 31, 2005. "Arthur Andersen Conviction Overturned." *CNN.com.* http://www.cnn.com/2005/LAW/05/31/scotus.arthur.andersen/, accessed October 19, 2021.

Molot, Jonathan T. April 2, 2009. "A Market in Litigation Risk." *University of Chicago Law Review* 76(1): Article 13.

Moohr, Geraldine Szott. April 2004. "Prosecutorial Power in an Adversarial System: Lessons from Current White-Collar Cases and the Inquisitorial Model." *Buffalo Criminal Law Review* 8(1): 165–220.

Moon, John. July 21, 2016. Personal Interview.

Morgensen, Gretchen. August 26, 2007. "Inside the Countrywide Lending Spree." *New York Times.* https://www.nytimes.com/2007/08/26/business/yourmoney/26country.html, accessed October 4, 2017.

Morgensen, Gretchen, Louise Story. April 14, 2011. "In Financial Crisis, No Prosecutions of Top Figures." *New York Times*.

Mulvihill, Geoff. December 17, 2020. "WATCH: Sackler Family Members Who Own Purdue Testify before Congress." *Associated Press*, accessed August 15, 2021.

New York State Attorney General. December 5, 2006. *Countrywide Agrees to New Measures to Combat Racial and Ethnic Disparities in Mortgage Loan Pricing.* https://ag.ny.gov/press-release/2006/countrywide-agrees-new-measures-combat-racial-and-ethnic-disparities-mortgage, accessed October 5, 2021.

New York University Law School. April 29, 2019. "Andrew Weissman Returns to NYU Law." https://www.law.nyu.edu/news/andrew-weissmann-center-administration-criminal-law, accessed October 19, 2021.

Noguchi, Yuki. September 2, 2014. "What's in a Name? Former Arthur Andersen Employees Spell It Out." *NPR.* http://www.npr.org/2014/09/02/344983151/whats-in-a-name-former-arthur-anderson-employees-spell-it-out, accessed August 18, 2015.

Office of Inspector General, Justice Department. *The External Effects of the Federal Bureau of Investigation's Reprioritization Efforts.* Audit Report 05–37. https://oig.justice.gov/reports/FBI/a0537/chapter1.htm#13, Accessed September 7, 2020.

Office of Personnel, Pay & Leave Salaries & Wages, Salary Table No. 2014-ES Management https://www.opm.gov/policy-data-oversight/pay-leave/salaries-wages/salary-tables/14Tables/exec/html/ES.aspx.

Olson, Mancur. 1982. *The Rise and Decline of Nations: Economic Growth, Stagflation and Social Rigidities.* New Haven: Yale University Press.

Oppel Jr., Richard A. and Don Van Natta Jr. January 12, 2002. "Enron's Collapse: The Relationships; Bush and Democrats Disputing Ties to Enron." *New York Times*, https://www.nytimes.com/2002/01/12/business/enron-s-collapse-the-relationships-bush-and-democrats-disputing-ties-to-enron.html, accessed April 7, 2018.

Perino, Michael. 2010. *The Hellhound of Wall Street: How Ferdinand Pecora's Investigation of the Great Crash Forever Changed American Finance.* New York: Penguin Press.

Persky, Anna Stolley. May 1, 2010. "Aggressive Justice." *American Bar Association Journal*. https://www.abajournal.com/magazine/article/aggressive_justice, accessed October 19, 2021.

Peters, Jeremy W. and Simon Romero. July 5, 2006. "Enron Founder Dies before Sentencing." *New York Times*. https://www.nytimes.com/2006/07/05/business/05cnd-lay.html, accessed April 7, 2018.

Poindexter, Carol. August 2016. "Criminal and Civil Liability for Corporations, Officers and Directors." *Practical Law*. Accessed online, chrome-extension://efaidnbmnnnibpcajpcglclefindmkaj/https://www.nortonrosefulbright.com/-/media/files/nrf/nrfweb/imported/20160801---criminal-and-civil-liability-for-corporations-officers-and-directors.pdf.

Polantz, Katelyn. July 5, 2015. "Holder's Return to Covington Was Six Years in the Making." *The National Law Journal*.http://www.nationallawjournal.com/id=1202731265593/Holders-Return-to-Covington-Was-Six-Years-in-the-Making, accessed August 19, 2015.

Rakoff, Jed S. January 9, 2014. "Why Have No High-Level Executives Been Prosecuted in Connection with the Financial Crisis?" *New York Review of Books*. https://www.nybooks.com/articles/2014/01/09/financial-crisis-why-no-executive-prosecutions/, accessed August 24, 2020.

Rakoff, Jed S. November 21, 2016. Personal Interview.

Reckard, E. Scott. February 19, 2011. "Criminal Probe Dropped against Countrywide CEO Angelo Mozilo." *Washington Post*. https://www.washingtonpost.com/business/criminal-probe-against-countrywide-ceo-ends/2011/02/18/ABrbObJ_story.html, accessed August 1, 2017.

Renshon, Stanley. 2011. "Redemption, Fairness, and the Politics of Transformation in the Obama Presidency." *Political Psychology* 32(6): 1035–1057.

Richardson, Gary, Alejandro Komai, Michael Gou, and Daniel Park. "Stock Market Crash of 1929." *Federal Reserve History*. https://www.federalreservehistory.org/essays/stock_market_crash_of_1929, accessed August 7, 2017.

Rochabrun, Marcelo and Cezary Podkul. December 15, 2016. "The Fateful Vote That Made New York City Rents So High." *ProPublica*. https://www.propublica.org/article/the-vote-that-made-new-york-city-rents-so-high, accessed April 7, 2020.

Roe, Mark and Howell Jackson. 2009. "Public and Private Enforcement of Securities Laws: Resource-Based Evidence." *Journal of Financial Economics* 93: 207–238.

Savage, Charlie. May 24, 2012. "2 Prosecutors in Case of Senator Ted Stevens Are Suspended." *New York Times*. https://www.nytimes.com/2012/05/25/us/politics/2-prosecutors-in-case-of-senator-ted-stevens-are-suspended.html, accessed October 19, 2021.

Schattschneider, E. E., 1960. *The Semisovereign People: A Realist's View of Democracy in America*. New York: Holt, Rinehart and Winston.

Schmidt, Michael S. and Michael D. Shear. December 28, 2017. "Trump Says Russia Inquiry Makes U.S. 'Look Very Bad.'" *New York Times*. https://www.nytimes.com/2017/12/28/us/politics/trump-interview-mueller-russia-china-north-korea.html, accessed January 18, 2018.

Schwartz, Jonathan. February 25, 2016. “Securities 101: A Circuit Split in the Standard for Pleading Loss Causation in Securities Fraud Cases.” *American Bar Association.* http://apps.americanbar.org/litigation/committees/securities/articles/winter2016-0216-circuit-split-in-standard-for-pleading-loss-causation-securities-fraud-cases.html, accessed October 9, 2017

S.E.C. v. Mozilo, Sambol, Sieracki, CV09–03994, complaint.

Select USA. The Financial Services Industry in the United States. http://selectusa.commerce.gov/industry-snapshots/financial-services-industry-united-states, accessed August 5, 2015

Senate Permanent Subcommittee on Investigations Hearing Transcript. April 13, 2011. *Wall Street and the Financial Crisis: Anatomy of a Financial Collapse.* https://www.hsgac.senate.gov/imo/media/doc/PSI%20REPORT%20-%20Wall%20Street%20&%20the%20Financial%20Crisis-Anatomy%20of%20a%20Financial%20Collapse%20(FINAL%205-10-11).pdf, accessed August 24, 2020.

Sherter, Alain. September 10, 2010. “No Time: Feds Have Given Up Trying to Send Bankers to Jail.” *CBS News.* https://www.cbsnews.com/news/no-time-feds-have-given-up-trying-to-send-bankers-to-jail/, Accessed July 26, 2021.

SIGTARP. January 27, 2017. *Special Inspector General Trouble Asset Relief Program Report to Congress.* https://www.sigtarp.gov/sites/sigtarp/files/Quarterly_Reports/January_27_2017_Report_To_Congress.pdf, accessed July 27, 2021.

Smith, Martin, Linda Hirsh, andBen Gold. “The Untouchables.” *PBS Frontline.* January 22, 2013. http://www.pbs.org/wgbh/pages/frontline/business-economy-financial-crisis/untouchables/transcript-37/, accessed August 19, 2015.

Skowronek, Stephen. 1993. *The Politics Presidents Make; Leadership from John Adams to Bill Clinton.* Cambridge, MA: Belknap Press.

Sorkin, Andrew Ross. 2010. *Too Big to Fail.* Harlow, England: Penguin Books.

Sorkin, Andrew Ross and Mary Williams Walsh**.** February 4, 2013. U.S. Accuses S. & P. of Fraud in Suit on Loan Bundles. *New York Times.* http://dealbook.nytimes.com/2013/02/04/u-s-and-states-prepare-to-sue-s-p-over-mortgage-ratings/?ref=business&_r=0, accessed January 2015.

Spitzer, Elliot. December 5, 2006. Press Release: *Countrywide Agrees to New Measures to Combat Racial and Ethnic Disparities in Mortgage Loan Pricing.* https://ag.ny.gov/press-release/countrywide-agrees-new-measures-combat-racial-and-ethnic-disparities-mortgage-loan, accessed October 9, 2017.

Stemen, Don and Bruce Frederick. 2012. *Rules, Resources, and Relationships: Contextual Constraints on Prosecutorial Decision Making.* http://works.bepress.com/don_stemen/1, accessed October 26, 2015.

Stephanopoulos, George and Aaron Katersky. September 12, 2022. “Justice Department Pressured Former US Attorney to Bring Cases against Trump Enemies, Geoffrey Berman Says.” *ABC News.* https://abcnews.go.com/Politics/justice-department-pressured-us-attorney-bring-cases-trump/story?id=89745338.

Stevenson, Jonathan. May 15, 2020. “With Flynn, Barr Burns Justice to Feed Trump’s ‘Obamagate’ Fantasy.” *New York Review of Books.* https://www.nybooks.com/daily/2020/05/15/with-flynn-barr-burns-justice-to-feed-trumps-obamagate-fantasy/, accessed May 16, 2020

Stewart, Jon. September 22, 2022. "A Former US Attorney on How Trump Politicized the DOJ." *The Problem, with Jon Stewart* podcast. https://www.audacy.com/podcasts/the-problem-with-jon-stewart-62789/a-former-us-attorney-on-how-trump-politicized-the-doj-1526403865.

Stratmann, Thomas. March 19, 2002. "Can Special Interests Buy Congressional Votes? Evidence from Financial Services Legislation." *The Journal of Law and Economics* 45(2): 345–373.

Suskind, Ron. 2011. *Confidence Men: Wall Street, Washington and the Education of a President.* New York: HarperCollins

Taibbi, Matt. 2014. *Divide; American Injustice in the Age of the Wealth Gap.* New York: Spiegel & Grau.

Thompson, Larry D. 2003. "Principles of Federal Prosecution of Business Organizations." (Thompson Memo.) U.S. Department of Justice. Office of the Deputy Attorney General.

Thornburgh, Richard Lewis. Justice Department Biography. http://www.justice.gov/ag/bio/thornburgh-richard-lewis, accessed October 20, 2015.

Treasury Department Report. April 2012. *The Financial Crisis Response in Charts.* United States Department of the Treasury. https://www.treasury.gov/resource-center/data-chart-center/Documents/20120413_FinancialCrisisResponse.pdf, accessed July 26, 2021.

Turk, Matthew C. 2017. "Regulation by Settlement." *Kansas Law Review* 66: 259–324.

Twitter.com/HillaryClinton.

Twitter.com/TheRealDonaldTrump.

The United States Attorney's Office, Eastern District of New York—Brooklyn, New York. May 25, 2013. FindLaw.

United States Financial Crisis Inquiry Commission. 2011. *The Financial Crisis Inquiry Report: final report of the National Commission on the Causes of the Financial and Economic Crisis in the United States.*

United States Financial Crisis Inquiry Commission. 2011. *The Financial Crisis Inquiry Report: Final Report of the National Commission on the Causes of the Financial and Economic Crisis in the United States—Resource Library. https://fcic.law.stanford.edu/resource/graphics,* accessed July 27, 2021.

United States of America v. McGraw Hill Companies and Standard & Poor's Financial Services LCC, CV13–00779, complaint.

United States Senate, Subcommittee on Senate Resolutions 84 and 234. (*The Pecora Committee.*) https://www.senate.gov/about/powers-procedures/investigations/pecora.htm, accessed October 5, 2021.

U.S. v. Bank of American Corporation, successor to Countrywide Financial Corporation, 12 Civ 1422.

Valukas, Anton R. Jenner & Block—People. https://jenner.com/people/AntonValukas, accessed October 26, 2021.

Valukas, Anton R. April 6, 2011. Testimony of the examiner, Lehman Brothers Bankruptcy, Committee on Banking, Housing, & Urban Affairs Subcommittee on Securities, Insurance, and Investment United States Senate. https://www.banking

.senate.gov/imo/media/doc/ValukasTestimony4611am.pdf, Accessed August 24, 2020.

Wallance, Gregory J. "The Wall Street-Washington Revolving Door Is as American as Apple Pie." *Forbes.* http://www.forbes.com/sites/forbesleadershipforum/2013/03/14/the-wall-street-washington-revolving-door-is-as-american-as-apple-pie/, Accessed August 14, 2015.

Wasson, Reyna. December 5, 2016. "Negotiation Lessons from the Passage of the ACA." Fels Institute of Government at the University of Pennsylvania. http://www.fels.upenn.edu/recap/posts/negotiation-lessons-passage-aca, accessed October 9, 2017.

Waxman, Rep. Henry A. October 22, 2008. "Opening Statement of Chairman, Committee on Oversight and Government Reform Credit Rating Agencies and the Financial Crisis." https://oversight.house.gov/sites/democrats.oversight.house.gov/files/documents/20081022102221.pdf, accessed August 24, 2020.

Whitford, Andrew B. January 2002. "Bureaucratic Discretion, Agency Structure, and Democratic Responsiveness: The Case of the United States Attorneys." *Journal of Public Administration Research and Theory: J-PART* 12(1): 3–27.

Yates, Sally Quillian. September 9, 2015. *Individual Accountability for Corporate Wrongdoing.* Justice Department Memoranda. https://www.justice.gov/archives/dag/file/769036/download, accessed August 24, 2020.

Younglai, Rachelle and Sarah N. Lynch. April 13, 2011. "Credit Rating Agencies Triggered Financial Crisis, U.S. Congressional Report Finds." *Reuters.* http://www.huffingtonpost.com/2011/04/13/credit-rating-agencies-triggered-crisis-report_n_848944.html, accessed October 9, 2017.

Index

About the Author

Sari Krieger is a professor of political science at the University at Albany and the City University of New York. Her work focuses on American government, institutions and incentive structures. She has a PhD in political science from the City University of New York Graduate Center, a master's degree in political science from New York University, and a bachelor's degree in environmental policy from Binghamton University. She previously worked as a journalist covering government, business and law for more than a decade at *Dow Jones/the Wall Street Journal*, the *Financial Times Group, Consumer Reports* and local newspapers in New York, Virginia, and New Hampshire.

www.ingramcontent.com/pod-product-compliance
Ingram Content Group UK Ltd.
Pitfield, Milton Keynes, MK11 3LW, UK
UKHW041840031026
15587UKWH00002B/904

9 781793 654496